LEARNING FROM EACH OTHER / The Commonsense Way to Train Your Dog

LEARNING FROM EACH OTHER /The Commonsense Way to Train Your Dog

WILLIAM McGLINCHEY

HOWELL
BOOK HOUSE
New York

Maxwell Macmillan Canada
Toronto

Maxwell Macmillan International
New York   Oxford   Singapore   Sydney

Howell Book House
Macmillan Publishing Company
866 Third Avenue
New York, NY 10022

Maxwell Macmillan Canada, Inc.
1200 Eglinton Avenue East
Suite 200
Don Mills, Ontario M3C 3N1

Macmillan Publishing Company is part of the Maxwell Communication Group of Companies.

Library of Congress Cataloging-in-Publication Data
McGlinchey, William.
    Learning from each other : the commonsense way to train your dog /
William McGlinchey.
        p.   cm.
    Includes bibliographical references.
    ISBN 0-87605-659-1
    1. Dogs—Training.   I. Title.
SF431.M465   1991
626.7'0887—dc20   91-19831   CIP

Macmillan books are available at special discounts for bulk purchases for sales promotions, premiums, fund-raising, or educational use. For details, contact:

Special Sales Director
Macmillan Publishing Company
866 Third Avenue
New York, NY 10022

10 9 8 7 6 5 4 3 2 1

Printed in the United States of America

TO SANDY

She became the teacher
and I became the student

Contents

Part III: Trusting Each Other

Preface

MANY PEOPLE think obedience training is only for show dogs. It isn't. It's for any dog—the family dog, your best friend, the puppy you just fell in love with and the puppy that grew into a two-hundred-pound hulk capable of pulling you anywhere she wants to go. Most of all, training is for you, the dog's owner, because it enables you and your dog to get more enjoyment from each other.

Usually dog trainers teach dogs to perform in the obedience ring or to do what shows require. But just because a dog has a blue ribbon, that doesn't mean he knows how to behave at home or wherever you'd like to take him. Obedience training involves much more than pleasing a judge. It teaches you and your dog how to live together.

When I met Bill McGlinchey several years ago I had already taken my dog Kate to two obedience schools. We graduated with honors from the first one and barely escaped with our lives from the second. And we still didn't know anything.

The first school was monotonous. One night a week, for eight weeks, we spent an hour and a half going over the same basic commands to sit, stay, come and heel. We did them as we walked the perimeter of a huge gymnasium with about forty other dogs and their owners, barely able to hear the instructions of the "trainer" who stood in the middle of the room and had a voice that didn't carry. At her feet a Golden Retriever lay on her side and slept soundly throughout the lesson. "Is this what you want to achieve?" the "trainer" asked proudly, pointing to the inert animal as the first lesson ended. "It just takes time."

Actually, I didn't want an animal that wasn't interested in what was going on around her. Kate, a female German Shepherd Dog, was a year old then. She was lively and intelligent, and I wanted her to stay that way. But I also wanted to be able to control her, and I couldn't. If anything, she was controlling me. For at least an hour every day we practiced what we had learned in class—sit, stay, heel, come. Sometimes Kate obeyed me; sometimes she didn't. As time went on, more often she didn't. She knew there wasn't much I could do about it. Pulling on the lead meant nothing to her. She was stronger than I was, and if she didn't want to move, she didn't.

In class we got a lot of praise. "It just takes time," the "trainer" repeated when I expressed concern that I would never be able to control Kate without a lead. We were often singled out as model students, and when we graduated after eight weeks we were on the "honor roll." But I knew we weren't nearly as good as the "trainer" said we were.

Then I enrolled in another school, one with a pretty uppity reputation. The first lesson was a "get-acquainted" affair, and Kate and I were told to wear matching bandanas around our necks. "The dogs really enjoy it," the registrar assured me.

The class met in another gymnasium, but it was small and there were more than fifty dogs and their owners present. Square-dance music blasted from a loudspeaker and we were told to form two lines facing each other.

"Now we're going to dance with our dogs," a man shouted over the din. "We're going to do a Virginia reel—the dogs love it!"

Kate had been apprehensive from the moment we entered the gym. At first glance, it seemed to me that none of the other dogs had any kind of training. They pulled on their leads and lunged at each other, confused by so many strangers. Their owners seemed oblivious to the potential danger and stood in small groups, chatting as if they were at a cocktail party. All the dogs and their owners wore matching bandanas around their necks.

"Now," bellowed the man I couldn't see, "you people at the beginning of each line, step away from your dog and stand facing him. Hold the lead up as high as you can. That's right, hold your arm *way* up high! Now—everybody else is going to skip, *with their dog,* under those held-up leads while the music plays! Okay, now, Virginia reel!"

Kate looked at me and I swear I could read her mind. She wondered whether I was losing mine. The woman at the beginning of our line was short and had a Pekingese—Kate and I would have to crouch down to walk under the lead. The Pekingese wouldn't sit still and was already nipping anxiously at the first dog that approached. I knew we never would make it without an incident.

"Kate, heel!" I said, turning toward an exit. For once, Kate fell right in beside me and we left. On our way out I took off those silly bandanas and threw them in a trash can. I didn't even want to be reminded of what we had almost done.

The next morning I called my dog's breeder, who had recommended the two schools. "I want a *professional* trainer!" I said. "I don't want to waste any more of my time."

That's how I got Bill McGlinchey's name. People who are serious about dog training know who he is, and some judges at obedience trials can spot a McGlinchey-trained dog by its superior performance. But Bill doesn't have much patience with people who just want to go through the motions of training, so serious people know better than to refer the casual dog owner to him.

"I'm hardly casual," I told the breeder. "I'm desperate. My dog is starting to train *me!*"

"Wel-l-l, you can give Bill a call," the breeder said. "Tell him I sent you."

I had to call Bill McGlinchey four times before he gave Kate and me an appointment. I knew he was busy, but I also suspected he was putting me to the test: Was I serious about training my dog? "Let me take a look at her first," he said when he agreed to meet us. "Then we'll see about lessons." That made sense.

It was a forty-mile ride to his house, and light snow was falling as Kate and I started out, but I wasn't about to let anything stop us. I had the feeling that I would never get another appointment if I did.

He was waiting for us in his driveway when we arrived. He was dressed for the cold, with hat and gloves, and I had the feeling that underneath the bulky clothes was a powerfully built man. He wore tinted glasses and had a round Irish face that should have been laughing but wasn't. His expression was noncommittal.

I parked the car several feet from where he stood and got out. Kate was in the backseat and I pushed my seat forward to let her get past. I had left her lead attached to her collar (something I later learned never to do) and I took hold of it quickly, trying to demonstrate that we weren't exactly beginners. I commanded her to heel, which she didn't do immediately but rather when she got around to it. Her attention was fixed on Bill, who said "Hello" and nothing more. He stayed where he was.

"Sit," I said to Kate, stopping a few feet in front of Bill. I introduced myself and we shook hands. Kate's ears were back, and I certainly wasn't proud of the way she was sitting. Her hips were slung to one side and she was slouching down as if she were trying to appear smaller. Then she stood up and pulled toward the car.

"What do you think?" I asked Bill, trying to pull her back.

"Show me what you've learned so far," he said.

I took Kate through the sit, stay, come and heel we had done thousands of times before. I didn't say "Down" because I knew she wouldn't do it.

"Well, at least you're consistent," Bill said. "Ever since you got out of the car, you've done everything wrong. You're not even holding the lead right."

And so Kate and I began the most enlightening, valuable education an animal and a human being can experience. We began to learn from each other how to get along in our world. Our basic training took a little longer than usual because we had to undo the mistakes of our past efforts. It was hard work; at times it was tedious. In the beginning it was often frustrating, but it was always fascinating and it could be fun. Our reward was a sense of communication and friendship between the two of us that is beyond what I ever thought possible. Kate feels confident about herself as a dog, and I feel pretty good about myself as a person. To this day, several years later, our understanding of each other continues to grow. It gives us both great pleasure.

What made it happen? The right kind of training.

For me, Bill McGlinchey took the mystery out of training my dog. There was a logical, practical reason for everything he taught us to do, a respect for both the needs of the person and the needs of the dog. Those are the qualities that distinguish him in his profession, and they are the goals of this book.

As a writer, I look at training as a means of communication

between Kate and me. You might even call it a language in itself, but one that includes much more than words. I am amazed at how many words my dog understands, but I am even more amazed by my ability to read her—the tension or relaxation of her body, the angle of her head, the position of her ears or her tail and, of course, the expression in her eyes. I can even read the many different ways she barks. I know, without looking, whether a friend or a stranger is approaching my door. I know when Kate's ready to play and when she's putting me on. While it is true that I have taught Kate how to adapt to my world, she has also brought her world into mine and made it a better place.

Let me assure anyone who thinks training inhibits a dog that it does exactly the opposite. The right kind of training respects the special qualities of a dog and makes it possible for the owner to develop them. That's why I was delighted when Bill McGlinchey agreed that his training methods could be demonstrated in a book. This will make it possible for many more people to experience what I have learned with his help: the unique pleasure that comes from sharing life with a remarkable animal.

Phyllis Hobe
East Greenville, Pennsylvania

PART I

GETTING TO KNOW YOUR DOG

1

A Commonsense Approach to Training

SOME PEOPLE go into obedience training because they want to show their dogs in competition. Some go into it because they are having problems with their dogs. Both are valid reasons for a person and a dog to spend the time and effort that training demands. Proper training can bring out the best in your dog if you intend to show him, and it can solve problems that are making you and your dog miserable. But the best reason for anyone to go into obedience training is to teach his dog acceptable everyday behavior. This includes what your dog is allowed to do in your home; which section of the yard is out of bounds because your garden is there; how to get in and out of an elevator; how to ride in your car; how to walk down the street by your side, stopping at corners and waiting for your command to cross a busy street and, in general, how to adapt to your life-style so that the two of you can enjoy the time you spend together.

Training a dog has to make sense—not only to the person but also to the animal. For instance, there's no point in teaching a dog to come to you by pulling him toward you, because when you pull one way, the dog instinctively pulls the opposite way. You are just going to end up with a test of strength. If the dog is small, you'll win, but what you are teaching the dog is that when you say, "Rover, come!" he is going to be dragged somewhere. If the dog is large and you can't get him to budge, you are teaching him that you have no control over him. So far, you haven't done anything to teach him what you really want him to do—which is to come to you and sit squarely in front of you as soon as you give the command.

Instead of pulling the dog toward you, try something that will make sense to both of you. The dog is sitting, and you're facing him at the end of the lead. If you are holding the lead properly (see chapter 6), you can easily give it a quick snap—a brisk jerk toward you—and then release the pressure immediately. This doesn't hurt the dog, but it startles him enough to get his attention. At the same time, call the dog's name, pause briefly and give the command "Come" in an authoritative tone of voice. By doing this, you are signaling to the dog what you want him to do, but you are giving him the choice of doing it or being signaled again. He'll probably refuse to obey the first few times, so you snap the lead again—lightly and quickly—until he decides that it is easier to come to you. And animals always take the easy way out. When you praise him for obeying the command, he'll be more willing to do it again.

THE VALUE OF TRAINING

I think all dogs should be trained, for the good of the animal, the owner, their neighbors and the community. Training develops the tremendous potential for learning that all dogs have. It also helps the dog to adapt to the society he has to live in.

If human beings had to live in the dog's society, we wouldn't have such things as concrete sidewalks, buildings, shopping malls, paved roads or automobiles. We'd have to learn how to live in the woods, and our survival skills wouldn't compare to those of the dog. We'd have to learn from him. In our society, the dog has to learn from us, and a trained dog stands a better chance of surviving because he has learned how to live by the rules that govern the lives of human beings. The dog that hasn't been taught how to live by our rules is put in jeopardy by his owner.

Training has a lot to offer the owner, too. If you think you are superior to the dog, you are wrong. The dog has keener senses and makes better use of them than you do of yours, and you can learn a lot about yourself, your life and your world from working with him. The psychological makeup of the dog is different from that of the human being. You'll never find a person who is so loving, so forgiving, so attentive to your likes and dislikes. Dogs are very open about their emotions, whereas most people cover them up, but working with your dog can make you more comfortable about expressing your own feelings.

Training is more than a method of solving behavior problems. It is more than giving and executing commands. Training sets the ground rules for a compatible relationship between you and your dog. It is a learning experience for both of you. After a while you don't even have to see that your dog is carrying out a command. You know he is, and he knows he is doing what he's supposed to do. That's a beautiful feeling.

THE DIFFERENCE BETWEEN OBEDIENCE AND SUBMISSION

Sometimes people are reluctant to train their dogs because they are afraid it will break their spirit. That isn't true. Training, if done properly, gives a dog self-confidence and pride in his accomplishments. Once he and the owner get past the tedium and repetition of the early lessons, the dog goes through the exercises eagerly. He responds to commands with trust and enthusiasm. He takes corrections without getting discouraged or fearful, and the relationship between him and his owner is close and caring.

A submissive dog is one that has been improperly trained and overcorrected. He will often cringe, cower, fall on the floor and crawl on his stomach when his owner gives a command. Corrections terrify or depress him.

Obedience training never was meant to break a dog's spirit. It simply gives you control over your dog so that the two of you can work as a team. Good training takes into account the breed of the dog as well as his individual temperament. Corrections are made to clarify a command, not to intimidate the dog, and they should always be followed by a command to do something that will earn the dog praise for doing it properly.

MUTUAL APPRECIATION:
THE MENTAL AND PHYSICAL RELATIONSHIP
BETWEEN PERSON AND DOG

Training a dog is like anything else. There are only three ways to get better at it: *practice, practice, practice.* In the beginning it is a struggle for both the person and the dog. Doing the basic exercises over and over until you get them right is often tedious, frustrating and boring. But it gets better and easier if you stick with it. At some point, if you've become involved with your dog and have practiced with him regularly, everything the two of you do will be right. You will know it when it happens. You will have a wonderful sense of accomplishment, and your attitude will travel straight down the lead to your dog.

On the other hand, if you have a sluggish attitude when you work with your dog, if you really don't want to be training him or if you'd rather be doing something else, that will go down the lead to the dog, too, and he won't work well. Naturally you won't be enthusiastic every single time you work with your dog—and neither will he—but if you can motivate yourself to make your best effort, no matter what your mood, your dog will perform better.

TAKING THE MYSTERY OUT OF TRAINING

People frequently ask me, "How long will it take to train my dog?" My answer is, "That depends upon you."

If you are willing to work diligently, and if you can set aside a certain amount of time to work each day, you can train your dog to do any one of the basic exercises in seven days. In two months you should have a dog trained in basic Subnovice (on-lead) exercises. If you cut short your working time when you are frustrated or when your dog isn't performing well, or if you can't work with him every day, training will take longer.

Working too hard with your dog and trying to train him faster isn't a good idea. It takes time for the basic mechanics to become automatic for both of you.

My advice is to use the instructions in Parts II and III as if you were attending classes. Work on a seven-day basis. Learn the mechanics of an exercise on the first day and then practice them for the next six days. At the beginning of your working time each day, review the mechanics of the exercises you learned the previous weeks. Review is an important part of the training process. It can also be encouraging to you and your dog, because while you may be performing the new exercise awkwardly, you will be able to see that you are doing the previous exercises more fluidly.

Make it your goal to perform each new exercise perfectly by the seventh day. Imagine that you are in a class with other students and their dogs, all of whom have worked very hard during the past week. Consider how you will feel if you and your dog aren't prepared to be at your best. Believe me, if you haven't practiced, it will show. I've trained thousands of dogs and their owners, and I can always tell when someone hasn't done his homework.

Don't blame your dog's poor performance on him. Sometimes, when people see a dog that is performing better than theirs, they will jump to the conclusion that breed has something to do with it. Some breeds of dogs are easier to train than others. Some respond positively to authority and some wilt under it. There are also differences within the breed itself, because dogs, like people, are individuals. You have to adjust your handling to the dog's temperament. But the success of your training doesn't depend upon your dog. It depends upon you and the amount of effort you are willing to put into it, especially in the beginning.

Years ago a man came to one of my classes with the homeliest German Shepherd I had ever seen, but his owner thought he was the most terrific dog in the world. And that's the way the man worked with him. By the end of the on-lead and off-lead classes, both owner and dog worked beautifully and with great enthusiasm. Eventually the dog went on to get his Utility Dog degree. He took top honors in every show he entered. Both dog and owner loved every minute of their work. They were what every dog and owner should be: a team. That's what training is all about.

FORMAL AND INFORMAL TRAINING:
USING WHAT YOU LEARN

While the training maneuvers you will practice with your dog may at times seem strange and unnecessary, they will make sense later when you put them into practice. When you are learning them, they seem exaggerated and dramatic, but there is always a logical reason for doing them in a precise manner. When I'm asked by students, "Why does my dog have to heel at my side? Can't he walk a little ahead of me?" my answer is, "When your dog is off-lead, he belongs at your side where you have control over him. In that position he can read your body language and know exactly what you are going to do, because that's the way you've trained together. If your dog is heeling two feet ahead of you, how can he read you?"

Don't confuse heeling with a leisurely stroll with your dog off-lead in an area where you can safely allow him to walk ahead of you and stop to investigate his world. That's a walk. It is not a command. Heeling is an entirely different experience. It is a command that gives you control over the dog and tells him to pay attention to you.

Whatever your reason for training may be—whether it is to help your dog adapt to a civilized world, to enter him in competition, to solve a behavior problem or simply to learn how to enjoy him—take your training seriously. If you are casual about the exercises, if you are not willing to practice each one until you and your dog get it right, you will never reach the point where the two of you become a team. Aim at perfection. Give it everything you've got, and your dog will do the same. Then the hard part will be behind you and you will start having fun.

2

Do You Really Want a Dog?

BEFORE we go any farther, I am going to try to talk you out of getting a dog, because unless you *really* want one, you are better off without one. So is the dog.

A while ago I saw a TV commercial that was all too typical. It showed a big, sad-faced dog sitting on the back step of a house on a cold winter night. In the background was a lighted window and inside the house people were having a good time. Then someone said, "Whatever happened to that cute little puppy you had?" And someone answered, "Well, that cute little puppy grew up to be a big dog, so now he's outside."

Don't buy a dog on a whim. Often people think of all the fun they will have with a dog and they go out and buy a rhinestone collar before they even buy the dog. You will have more than fun with a dog; you will have a lot of responsibility. Maybe you'd love to cuddle a puppy in your arms, but remember that you will also have to housebreak him and feed him a few times a day. You will need a place in your house, such as a kitchen or a recreation room, with a vinyl or tile floor. If every inch of your apartment or house is covered with carpet, where will you raise your puppy while you are housebreaking him? If you are away all day, you can't expect a puppy to get along without going outdoors to relieve himself. Who will feed him while you are away?

Once you get a puppy, or even a grown dog, and find you can't take care of him, it will be very painful to give him up to someone else. That is why it is important to consider the negatives as well as the positives of dog ownership before you get one.

I don't believe everyone should own a dog. I've seen too many dogs that were acquired as puppies because they were irresistible and then spend the rest of their lives in a basement, a corner of the living room or the backyard because they required attention their owners weren't able to give them. There is nothing wrong with not wanting to own a dog. You may, in fact, be expressing your love for dogs by deciding that you don't have the time or the energy to take care of one. But there are many important things to consider if you do want one.

SOME DISADVANTAGES OF OWNING A DOG

Cost

Buying a dog from a reputable breeder can be expensive, and that is only the beginning. To protect your investment and because you care about the animal, you will want to feed him the most wholesome, nutritious food you can find, and that isn't cheap. Dogs, like people, require regular medical care: shots, checkups and attention to special or seasonal problems. Are you willing to take on this much financial responsibility?

Physical Characteristics

All dogs shed. Short-coated, dark-colored breeds only appear to shed less. Will all those hairs on your carpet and furniture be a problem?

If you are a person who can't stand to see a dog slobber, don't get a breed such as a St. Bernard or a Boxer. Consider another breed.

16

Time

A dog, especially a puppy, requires a lot of time and attention. He needs to be fed, taken out, exercised, played with and trained. If he isn't given time and attention, he will turn into a nuisance. Do you have enough time to own a dog? Do you have enough patience to give him your attention on a regular basis?

Living Space

What size house or apartment do you have? That is an important consideration. Don't make your decision according to the size of the dog. Not all large breeds need a lot of living space, and not all small breeds do well in efficiency apartments. St. Bernards do well in apartments, but Beagles do not. A breed's level of activity is more important than its size when it comes to choosing the right dog for your living space.

Climate

While dogs will adapt to any climate, different breeds do better in some climates than in others. If you live in a warm southern climate but you have your heart set on getting an Alaskan Malamute, a breed that is perfectly comfortable in temperatures well below zero, don't expect the dog to behave typically. It won't exhibit the energy it takes to pull a sled; instead, it will do what any other dog does in hot weather: lie down and take it easy.

Exercise

By now we all know that exercise is important to a healthy life, and this is true for dogs as well as people. It is not enough to take a dog out only to relieve himself and then come right back inside. Some dogs require more exercise than others, so you really ought to give serious thought to this before you decide to get a dog. Not many people have the kind of property where they can let the dog out to run and know that he is protected. Most dog owners have to take their dogs out for regular walks, no matter what the weather. If you want a dog that requires a great deal of exercise, you may have to consider getting up a half hour earlier each morning to exercise the dog. Is this something you are willing to do?

Exercising your dog in all kinds of weather

Playtime

Personal Life-style

If you like to travel, think about whether or not you will want to take your dog with you. It is hard to find hotels that will accommodate dogs, and it takes a lot of time to plan for your dog's food and water along the way. It is almost as hard to find an acceptable kennel to care for your dog if you decide not to take him with you. Getting someone to live in your house and take care of your dog while you are away is a more agreeable form of care, but it will cost more money.

If you work all day and have to leave the dog alone, are you willing to come home at lunchtime to take the dog out for a walk, or arrange for someone else to do it? Are you willing to come home after work and feed your dog, take him out and spend some time with him before you go to dinner with friends?

SOME ADVANTAGES OF OWNING A DOG

There are as many reasons for having a dog as there are dogs.

Companionship

A dog is good company and lots of fun. He's a good listener when you want to talk to someone, and being responsible for him will make you feel better about yourself. If you are at the stage in your life where you can take the time to walk through the woods with your dog, you will experience one of the great pleasures in life. If you prefer to stay home and read a book or watch TV, your dog will be happy just to be with you.

Protection

Dogs are an excellent early-warning system. They can smell smoke before you do, and their very presence may deter intruders.

Satisfaction

Maybe you've wanted a dog for years but weren't able to fit one into your life until now. If you've always been drawn toward a particular breed, this is the time to do some research and find out if it is the right one for you.

ENRICHING EACH OTHER'S LIFE

The most rewarding part of training your dog is the emotional involvement that develops between the two of you. Put very simply, it is the feeling of pleasure each of you gets from being with the other. Today the pace of daily life is so fast that most of us don't take time to stop and appreciate the good things around us. Having a dog can help you catch up on what you've been missing.

Some of the most enjoyable moments of my life have been those I have spent with Trapper, my German Shepherd. One day recently he and I were walking up a steep country road, something we do almost every morning. Trapper was a little ahead of me, pausing now and then to investigate a scent, and my mind was on all the things I had to do that day. I wasn't paying attention to my surroundings or the weather; it was just another busy day. Then, as Trapper moved out of the shade of a tree into the sunlight, I suddenly saw him as if for the first time. I was struck by the sheer beauty of the animal, by his strong features, his muscular neck and shoulders, the rhythm of his movement, the sunlight glistening off his coat—and suddenly the pressures of my daily life went away. I saw that it was a beautiful morning and the trees were coming into their autumn colors. Later on I would do some or all of the things I planned to do, but for the moment I was in touch with a more important world, the world of nature. By the time we came home, I was thoroughly relaxed.

INTERACTING: WHAT YOUR DOG CAN TEACH YOU ABOUT IT

Interacting with animals helps us to interact with people. Animals are much more tolerant of human shortcomings than we are. They don't try to change us. They do try to understand us.

If you really want to appreciate the animal you own, sometimes you have to stop what you are doing, forget about yourself, your job or your problems, and simply enjoy the animal and his world. Make some time for the two of you to share, whether you are jogging, walking or sitting on a park bench down the block from your apartment. If you are willing to get emotionally involved with your dog and look at life through his eyes, he can teach you how to be a better, more compassionate human being.

Forgiveness

How often do you feel hurt because you asked someone a simple question and got a short answer? How often do you feel rejected because you did something thoughtful and it wasn't appreciated? What do you do when these things happen? Do you carry a grudge? Try to get even?

A dog is more forgiving of human errors. If he comes up to you with his favorite toy in his mouth when you are not in the mood to play, you may brush him off with a "Go lie down!" and he will do it. But as soon as you are ready to play or spend some time with him, he's delighted.

If someone were to leave you at home for hours, you might be pretty angry by the time that person came home. But not your dog. Put your key in the door and you can already hear his tail banging against the floor or the wall, and the moment you walk in the door he is telling you how glad he is to see you.

Tolerance

Maybe you have had a bad day and you want to be left alone. Yet when you try to bury your head in a newspaper, your dog comes over and tries to get your attention. This may be something he has done for years and you've always found it lovable, but right now you are not in the mood for it and you reprimand him. Then you may realize that the dog didn't do anything wrong. He offered you companionship and pleasure, which may be why you wanted a dog. Just because you weren't in the mood to reciprocate, that is no reason to brush him off. You may feel like a fool for being so impatient, and if you do—Congratulations! Your dog is teaching you tolerance, not only for him but for the other people in your life. The next time someone brushes you off, maybe you won't be so unforgiving. Maybe you will realize that the person might have had a bad day, and you won't hold a grudge.

ARE YOU WILLING TO MAKE SOME CHANGES?

Bringing a dog into your life means you may have to make some changes in it. Some people call them sacrifices. But, then, love is often a matter of making sacrifices.

If you want a dog to stay out of your way, to lie in a corner of your living room or your basement and come out only when you are in the mood to be with him, then you are better off buying a painting or an ornament for your mantelpiece. But if you are willing to give a dog some of your time, your patience and understanding, if you can appreciate the kind of devotion a dog will unquestioningly give to you, you won't be sacrificing anything. You will be getting a lot in return.

3

Matching the Dog and
the Person

THERE'S AN OLD SAYING that people get to look like their dogs, or vice versa. Actually it makes some sense. You and your dog don't have to look like each other, but it is important for you to have a lot in common. If you like dogs and your dog likes people, that isn't enough to assure compatibility.

When a client tells me, "I can love any dog," my answer is, "Yes, but which one can you live with?" Loving a dog means spending a lot of time with him, and if you aren't compatible, you won't be happy together. Don't assume that you can turn any dog into exactly the kind of animal you want him to be. It doesn't work any better with dogs than it does with people. Dogs, like people, have individual characteristics that can't be changed, so it makes sense to choose a dog with characteristics similar to your own. Put at least as much study and effort into buying a dog as you would into buying a car. Hopefully, the dog will be with you much longer than a car and will play a much more important role in your life.

What many people mean when they say they "love" a dog is that they like the way a certain kind of dog looks. Or, if a certain breed of dog seems to be popular, they think they ought to love it because so many other people do. Sometimes they just love dogs in general and they think all dogs are alike.

Dogs are as different from each other as people are. But their differences are easier to identify because they are bred into the animals. In fact, the way a dog looks is the result of what he was bred to do. I'm not making a pitch for the purebred dog, because I have trained many excellent mixed-breed dogs. But there is something to be said for a dog of a recognizable breed because then you know what to expect in terms of intelligence, physical characteristics and behavior.

Even within a breed, dogs will vary. When a particular dog becomes very popular, a lot of people begin to breed carelessly. They are more interested in making a profit than in preserving the breed's qualities, and their dogs don't look or behave the way they should. That is why it is important to buy your dog from a reputable breeder. If you don't know of any, you can call the American Kennel Club and ask for a referral to breeders in your area. But don't stop there. Look at the puppies, then look at their sire and dam. Don't be intimidated by a puppy's papers. Ask some questions about his forebears. If possible, talk to some people who bought puppies from a previous litter. Ask the breeder what the breed's weak points are.

Many so-called "backyard breeders" can offer good dogs. If you are dealing with one, bring someone along who is knowledgeable in the breed. You should also have your veterinarian examine a puppy before you buy it. A breeder who is careful and conscientious should have no objection to these precautions, and they may save you some problems in the future.

LET'S TALK ABOUT LIVING SPACE

If you don't learn the facts about the whole dog, you may be in for some unpleasant surprises. That lovable little Irish Wolfhound puppy you just couldn't resist is going to grow into a 150-pound dog that needs far more room to run than your efficiency apartment offers. If you really have your heart set on a big dog, yet you are not athletic and don't want to give up your apartment, think about getting a St. Bernard. As big as he is, a St. Bernard does very well in an apartment because he doesn't need strenuous exercise. Just getting his huge body up on his feet, lying down again and going up

26

and down stairs is a lot of work for him. Naturally, he needs exercise, but a St. Bernard is not the kind of dog that needs to run around. Normal walks will keep him in shape.

On the other hand, if you want a small dog for a small amount of living space, don't make the mistake of getting a Beagle. He may be small, but he needs the outdoors and plenty of exercise. The Beagle is a hunting dog with a fine sense of smell. You don't necessarily have to go hunting to make him happy or to see him at his best, but you have to be willing to spend time outdoors with him and let him pick up some scents he can follow. If you enjoy hiking, he's the dog for you. But if you are a stay-at-home, you won't be comfortable with a dog that wants to go out all the time.

BREEDING MEANS MORE THAN LOOKS

Almost everyone has a favorite breed of dog, but if you ask people why, usually they will tell you that they like the way the dog looks, perhaps the way the dog looks when she moves. There is nothing wrong with appreciating a dog's appearance, but if a dog is going to become part of your family, you really ought to know more about her. Or, rather, more about what you can expect her to become.

Take the Irish Setter, for instance, one of the most beautiful dogs in the world. Years ago they became a favorite with many people because they liked the shiny, red-rust color of the coat and the way their long, fringed feathering flowed in the wind as they moved through a field. The dog became very popular as a house pet and was hardly ever used for the work she did best: hunting. An Irish Setter was bred to hunt. She doesn't take life seriously and she is always ready to play the kind of games that allow her to run full speed over long distances. She loves to chase and be chased, and she finds even the average backyard too confining. How is she going to get that kind of activity in a house or an apartment? No matter how much a family may love her or her looks, she is out of place in the average family home because nobody has the time or energy to take her out in the fields for a long run. And if the dog isn't able to use up her vast amount of energy—another aspect of her breeding—she will never calm down long enough for you to pet her. In her frustration, she may even become quite destructive of your property.

27

Consequently, the Irish Setter has become a dog many families would like to have but can't handle. She has gained a reputation for being high-strung, wacky and unstable—which isn't true. Take her out in the fields for a few hours and she is fine. She will be ready to come home and lie down all evening. But if you expect her to be a family pet and nothing else, she will drive you crazy.

The best way to choose a compatible breed is to do some research, not only about the whole dog, but also about yourself and your way of life. Read some books that describe typical breed traits in terms of behavior and personality characteristics (see the Bibliography for suggestions). Find out why a dog looks the way he does, why his appearance is a direct result of the work he was developed to perform. Then consider whether this animal's particular qualities can be adapted to your life right now. Visit a few dog shows and talk to some breeders and handlers. Make allowances for the fact that each one will tell you that his dog/breed is the best in the world. By this time you should be well past the point of falling in love with the first dog you see. Talk to some trainers, because they get to work with all kinds of breeds. If someone tells you that his dog/breed is wonderful, ask why and apply the answer to yourself and your life-style. A dog that is wonderful for someone else may turn out to be a problem for you. Or he may be exactly the kind of dog you need. Only you can decide.

CONSIDER WHAT THE DOG WAS BRED TO DO

Originally dogs were bred to perform certain functions that made them useful to human beings. Their physical characteristics, their behavior traits and even many of their instincts were developed over centuries to fit in with the way people lived long ago. Dogs helped us to farm, herd, hunt and explore. They protected us. Some even provided a means of transportation. At the same time they often gave us companionship in a world where isolation was much more common than it is today.

The way we live now is very different. Few of us have the kind of home or do the kind of work that requires the skills many dogs were bred to perform. We spend more time indoors than out. The dog was never bred to lie in a corner all day like an ornament or to dress up our property like a shrub. He is still a wonderful companion, but he was never bred to imitate a human being. His genes still carry specific qualities that need to be developed and expressed, but in ways that are acceptable in our modern world. And these qualities still influence the way the dog behaves.

For example, if you are thinking of buying a German Shepherd, ask yourself how much you really know about the breed. Maybe you are attracted by their intelligence, but did you know that they are also quite stubborn? While they are extremely versatile, they like to do things their own way. You have to earn their respect with time, patience and hard work. If you find that prospect stimulating, if you can enjoy a dog with a mind of her own and if you personally like to learn new things, then you will be comfortable with many of this breed's qualities. But the German Shepherd is a strong, active animal bred to herd sheep and cattle. That doesn't mean you have to live on a farm and keep livestock, but you do have to find ways to keep the dog exercised. German Shepherds can trot for hours and not get tired, and if you want to keep up with one, you had better be in shape—or plan to be.

Another characteristic of German Shepherds is a certain aloofness. They don't fall all over people when they first meet them. They like people, but they take their time appraising them. Once they decide they like someone, they are very friendly. If you prefer a dog that makes friends instantly and shows it, you might want to think about one of the retriever breeds.

When you are choosing a breed, don't think only in terms of recognized groups, such as Working Dogs, Sporting Dogs, Herding Dogs and so on. It is better to consider the specific breed's level of activity; in other words, how much space and exercise does the dog need? An Irish Wolfhound or a Scottish Deerhound needs a great deal of exercise and room to run, so they will not do well in an apartment in a metropolitan area, with a family that is out working all day and has no time to take them out of the city, regularly, to an area where they can do what they were bred to do. These dogs need to be with someone who enjoys exercising, has a lot of acreage and enough leisure time to spend outdoors with the dog. A Chihuahua, however, needs very little space to lead an active, healthy life and can be wonderful company for the person who isn't athletic.

The great outdoors

CONSIDER YOUR PERSONALITY AND LIFE-STYLE

Your characteristics count, too. You will be happier with a dog that fits in with your temperament and life-style.

If you like to jog with a dog at your side, don't choose an English Bulldog. He will never keep up with you. If you are an on-the-go person, get a dog that enjoys being active. If you are reflective, get a dog that enjoys just being with you while you are thinking. Will the dog's coat have to be clipped? Who's going to do it—you or a professional dog groomer?

Don't assume that you have to fit into a stereotype in order to have a dog. A house in the country is fine for some breeds, but others get along very well in cities. There are so many varieties of dogs that you can usually find one to fit into your way of life—as long as you are willing to invest some time into helping the dog to adapt.

You don't have to be young to own a dog. Personally I hope to have a dog for as long as I live, and I think it is unfortunate when people who like having a dog feel that they are getting too old for one. Several studies have shown that a dog is an excellent companion for the elderly. He keeps them from getting lonely, he is a wonderful listener, he gives them affection and taking care of him boosts a person's self-esteem.

While aging may limit our activity, it doesn't mean we can't have a dog. The solution lies in choosing a compatible breed. A few years ago I received a call from a woman who had just moved into a retirement community. She wanted me to train her and her new dog. She was well on in years and had always had a dog, so she wasn't about to give up such a pleasurable part of her life. "I used to have German Shepherds," she told me, "and I love the breed. But I don't have the energy to exercise such a large dog now, so I bought a Welsh Corgi."

It was a smart choice. A Welsh Corgi is a much smaller dog, but he is bred to herd, is extremely intelligent and has several other characteristics similar to the Shepherd's. If you become familiar with your breeds, you will find several that make excellent companions for senior citizens.

I don't advise a puppy for an elderly person because, whatever the breed, it isn't easy to keep up with one. But a fully grown dog of a compatible breed will adapt very well to the activity level of an older person. Some of the Toy breeds and the smaller terriers make excellent companions for older people, and they are easy to exercise.

Sometimes people with handicaps think they shouldn't own a dog because they can't give it enough exercise. But I know a bedridden man who took excellent care of a Chihuahua, and the dog made him look forward to each day. One room was all the space they needed. And if a person in a wheelchair is able to throw a ball a short distance, some of the terriers and the Toy breeds can get all the exercise they need chasing after it and bringing it back.

CONSIDER THE DOG'S AGE

The best dog I ever owned was a year and a half old when I bought her. She was a German Shepherd and was owned by a couple who bought her when she was a puppy and then didn't know what to do with her after she started to grow up. They both went to work all day and left the dog tied at the end of a long rope in their yard. When some neighborhood children went by the house, the dog would bark, and the children began to tease her. Eventually one of the children got too close to her and she bit the child—not badly, but enough to break the skin. The owners were concerned and decided to give up the dog.

I was looking for another dog at the time. Since dogs were my business, I had several of them, but I didn't have enough time to bring up a puppy. When I learned that a year-and-a-half-old German Shepherd was available I went to look at her. She had no training whatsoever, but I liked what I saw and arranged to buy her.

Training brought out Sandy's talents, which were considerable. She became the most remarkable dog I have ever known. She could do anything. She was completely obedience trained; she could also track and she could sniff out hidden drugs for law enforcement officers. She was great with children—mine and everybody else's. She lived to be eighteen and was active almost to the end. I feel very fortunate to have found her.

When most people think of getting a dog, they usually think in terms of a puppy. But a puppy requires special attention and a great deal of time, which you may not be able to give. An older dog may be a better choice for you.

If you go to work every day, you won't be able to give a puppy the care he needs. But, with a little sacrifice on your part, you can take good care of an older dog. A puppy eats several times a day and has to be taken out several times a day. A one- or a two-year-old dog usually is housebroken and eats one or two times a day. You can't just leave him home in the morning and come back sometime that evening; if that is what you have to do, then you really can't take care of a dog. But if you can make other arrangements (and we will talk about that in chapter 5, "When Training Begins"), you can accommodate a dog in your life.

YOUR DOG AND YOUR CHILDREN

I don't advise parents to get a dog for their children. I have seen the same thing happen too many times: the parents decide it would be nice for the kids to have a dog so that they can play with it and learn how to take care of an animal. For about two weeks the kids spend every waking minute with the dog—and then they lose interest in him because something else catches their attention. The parents are left to take care of the dog when that really isn't what they intended. So nobody is happy—not the parents, not the children and certainly not the dog.

I do advise parents who want a dog to get one *for themselves.* A dog fits into a family beautifully when the parents want him, when they choose a compatible dog and when they are willing to be responsible for him. He can also be a rewarding experience for a child, as a playmate and a teacher, as long as the child is encouraged to take on only the amount of responsibility a child can handle.

THE DOG YOU ALREADY HAVE

Up to this point I've been describing the ideal way to choose a dog. But that isn't the way most people and their dogs come together. Frankly, most people who come to me for training have chosen a dog out of impulse rather than research, and they have some of the problems that come from mismatching. Usually they aren't aware that incompatibility is the source of their problems, but when they realize it they always ask me, "Is there anything I can do about it?"

I can't give them a simple yes or no. First I have to ask them whether they really want the dog. If they do, are they willing to make some sacrifices for her? If they are, I tell them three things: "If you're willing to work with your dog, if you're willing to spend time with her and if you're willing to do exactly what I tell you to do—you'll both be okay."

Training can't work miracles, but it can make both you and your dog aware of your differences and what each of you will have to give up in order to reconcile them. That's the hard part. If you are as emotionally involved with your dog as she is with you, the rest is much easier. I see no reason why the two of you can't look forward to a long, mutually rewarding friendship.

4

Making a Commitment

WHEN YOU BRING a dog into your life, you don't know much about her and she knows nothing about you. She will get to know you, because that's her nature. If you will reciprocate and get to know her, you will find it one of the most valuable experiences you will ever have. Both of you will grow—physically, mentally and emotionally.

Training your dog is an excellent fitness workout. You will improve your coordination and use muscles you didn't know you had. One of my students came back to repeat Subnovice classes, even though she had done very well and gone on to Novice, because the exercise had helped her lose eleven pounds. You will also improve your ability to concentrate and focus your attention on a specific goal. As for your emotional well-being, there simply isn't any substitute for the emotional relationship a person can have with an animal. Even if you are the strong, silent type, you will become more expressive because the most important part of your communication with your dog will be your feelings.

THE ANIMAL–GOD RELATIONSHIP

It has been said that one of the big differences between a person and a dog is that the dog sees her god during her lifetime. That is the best way I know to explain what you mean to your dog. To her, life isn't going to get better some day. It is at its best right now—because you are here with her. She wants only to be with you, and whatever you choose to do is fine with her. Maybe she would like to play with a toy, but if you would rather read the newspaper, she will lie quietly by your side. If you want to do some errands, she would love to go along with you. If you can't take her, she will wait for you to come back and then give you a hero's welcome. If you want to go for a walk, she is ready—anywhere, anytime. She gives you her complete devotion.

You may have other important things going on in your life. Your dog has only one, and that is you. If you keep this distinction in mind, it will help you to understand how your dog looks at the world and how she responds to your behavior. Don't try to treat her as if she were a person. She isn't. She is an animal, and she deserves your respect.

YOUR NEEDS AND YOUR DOG'S

Because you are so important to your dog, she wants to please you. But you have to show her how—in ways she can understand. Communicating with her is not the same as communicating with a human being. She picks up information and meaning from observing your actions, not from hearing your words. Only when your words are synchronized with actions that are carefully repeated do your words actually come to mean something. For instance, if you are throwing a ball for your dog and she doesn't bring it back, don't stand there and tell her what a dummy she is. Think about it: Chasing a ball and bringing it back to you is a complicated process for a dog that never has done it. She sees only that you have thrown the ball away from you and has no idea what you mean when you shout, "Go get it!" No matter how many times you throw the ball and tell her to bring it back, she still won't get the message until you break the action down into steps and teach her one step at a time, praising her all along the way.

Training teaches you to speak the language of your dog. It makes you more aware of your own behavior as well as your dog's, so that you don't give a command with your voice and contradict it by the way you move. Once you begin to look at yourself through the eyes of your dog, you will understand how to tell her what you want her to do.

Your dog has certain physical needs that she depends on you to fulfill. She has to eat a certain amount of food a certain number of times every day. She has to go out and relieve herself at certain intervals. Sometimes you may have to put her needs before your own. If you come home from a bad day at work and all you want to do is eat and go to bed, you will have to put off your own gratification until you take your dog out, feed her and take her out again. But is that so difficult?

What about you? What do you need from your dog? That depends upon your reason for having a dog, and the reason will vary with the person. Some people like to get up and go out with a dog; some like to come home to a dog; some want a dog for protection; some want a dog to do a specific job, such as guarding property, helping them to overcome a handicap, or herding sheep. Most people, however, have a dog because they value the companionship, devotion and love the animal brings to their lives.

Whatever your reason for having a dog, you can teach her to do anything she needs to do to fit into your life comfortably. It will take time and effort, but the results are worth it.

BECOMING ATTENTIVE TO YOUR DOG

One of the basic rules of training is to pay attention to your dog. This is something your dog can teach you.

My dog knows my daily routine better than I do because he pays attention to me. Like most people, I don't pay great attention to things going on around me. I do things out of habit, while I'm thinking of something else. My dog, however, watches my body language because each move I make gives him a clue to what I'm going to do next.

When you begin to pay close attention to your dog, you will be amazed at how quickly you will learn to read her signals. She will do more than tell you when she wants to go out. Her body language will tell you when she is feeling sluggish, when she wants more exercise, when she is confused, when she is contented, when she is alarmed, when she needs some attention and affection and even when she is playing games with you.

Always take your dog's feelings into consideration. She won't be able to put them into words, the way a human being can, but if you care enough to pay close attention to her, you will soon learn to read her signals. Sometimes her feelings won't be the same as yours, and if you allow yourself to look at your surroundings through her eyes, you may save yourself some frustration. For example, if you were to take your young puppy out for a walk and you unsnapped the lead to give her a little freedom, the puppy would probably start to run around. Your neighborhood may not be new to you, but it is to your puppy. To her it is a whole new world, and she is a young animal with a lot of energy to burn off. After a few minutes, you may want to go home, so you call the dog. She ignores you. She sees another dog coming down the block and she runs off in that direction. You chase her and she runs faster. She is having a wonderful time exploring her new world and she wants to find out what that other animal is. Sure, you are upset, perhaps even embarrassed. You are also afraid that your puppy will run out into the street. But can you really expect her to come back to you when you haven't yet trained her to do it? When you finally apprehend her, you blame her, scold her, bring her home and refuse to have anything to do with her until you calm down. Your puppy knows that you are furious with her, but she doesn't understand why. You don't know how to explain it to her because you haven't yet learned how to communicate in a language she can understand.

Next time, try unsnapping the lead when you are in a confined area, such as a fenced yard or a portable exercise pen. You both will have a better time. You won't be worried about your dog's safety. Your dog will still have a big chunk of the world to explore on her own. And you can learn a few things by watching her.

Notice how she will suddenly turn around and scrutinize a blade of grass, sniffing it up and down its length. If you were to get down on your hands and knees, you probably wouldn't smell anything on that blade of grass. Nevertheless, it is a source of information to your dog because her sense of smell is so much keener than yours. Wherever you go with her, she will perceive more in the territory than you ever will. Notice how she will hear a truck rumbling down the road before you do. The more you observe her and see how she picks up signals you didn't even know were there, the more you will rely on her perceptions when you are with her. Her body language will tell you when something is coming—even whether it is a person or a thing. Her bark will tell you whether a friend or a stranger is at the door. Her curiosity will lead you to discover parts of the natural world you never used to notice.

LEARNING EACH OTHER'S LANGUAGE

If you were introduced into a group of people who were speaking a language you didn't understand, you wouldn't know what they were talking about if they told you to do something. When you begin to train your dog and you give her a command such as "Heel," you know what the word means, but your dog doesn't. In your mind, you can visualize that "Heel" means your dog should walk alongside you. Your dog can't. Her mind works in different ways. If you want her to walk alongside you, you have to show her what that means, physically. This doesn't mean your way of thinking is better than your dog's, because it isn't. It's just different, and that difference should always be taken into consideration when you are working with your dog.

While the basic training commands may seem arbitrary and rigid, they do have a purpose. Once again, put yourself back into a roomful of people speaking rapidly in a language unfamiliar to you. Confusing, isn't it? But if they were to repeat a few words over and over, and at the same time demonstrate physically what those words are telling you to do, you would soon understand what they mean. This is what you need to do with your dog: Repeat key words of a command and demonstrate to the dog, physically, what those words tell her to do.

The words themselves mean nothing. You can teach your dog to heel by repeating the word "kitchen" when you guide her into place by your side, and your dog will heel just as well, as long as you guide her correctly and always use the same word. The meaning of the command is conveyed to the dog by your consistency in using the key word, the proper action and an authoritative tone of voice. If you sing a command, as many well-meaning people will do, your dog probably won't pay attention to it because you don't sound as if you are in charge of the situation. If you give your command firmly, authoritatively, your dog will respond as if you know what you are doing.

HOW YOU REACT TO EACH OTHER

When I start a series of obedience classes, I look around and see people and dogs who don't know what to do with each other. They are confused and frustrated. By the time we go through basic obedience training, I look around and see teams of people and dogs who move as one, each half understanding what the other is doing. And they enjoy it.

Your training should be tailored to your individual needs and those of your dog. If you have a Border Collie, your verbal commands will often be enough to give you control over your dog because that breed is sensitive to correction. But if you have a Rottweiler, you will have to snap your lead with some of your commands because she will challenge your authority.

People often change themselves during training. If you are a soft-spoken person, you will need to practice speaking your commands sharply to get your dog's attention. If you are impatient and can't be bothered with details, you will have to learn how to put up with repetition and precision.

Once I had a student who was the most impatient man I'd ever met. He came into class with an Irish Setter that was very high-strung. While the man loved the dog, he simply wasn't able to give him the kind of careful, sustained, calm training he needed. The man would throw up his hands and walk away ten minutes after class began. "I'll never get it right," he insisted.

I began to work with the man and his dog for very short periods of time. As soon as I saw that they were getting restless, I ended the lesson. But the next time we would work a few minutes longer. The man followed the same procedure when he and his dog practiced at home between classes: He began by working only a few minutes, and as soon as he got impatient, he stopped. Each time, however, he worked just a little longer. Actually, he was conditioning himself to extend his patience a bit at a time. As he improved, so did his dog, and eventually they were able to work as long as the rest of the class. They learned more than Subnovice exercises in those classes; they learned how to be patient with each other. They lived near me, and for years I often saw them together when I drove past their home. The man had a lot of acreage and sometimes he'd be out in a field throwing sticks for his dog. Occasionally I'd see him sitting on the front steps next to his dog, both of them calmly watching the cars go by. They turned out to be a good match for each other.

Owning a dog is like living a life. You begin by not knowing much, and you make a lot of mistakes. But because you really care about your dog, you make it your business to gain some knowledge of her. She does the same with you. Pretty soon, that combination of knowledge and caring becomes an experience in genuine love. By doing things together and learning from each other, you will develop a mutual trust that will last throughout your relationship.

5

When Training Begins

THERE ARE TWO KINDS of training: formal and informal. Formal training is based on specific commands, exercises and goals, such as Sit, Stay, Down, etc. There are degrees of achievement, such as Companion Dog, Companion Dog Excellent, Utility Dog, Utility Dog Tracking and Utility Dog Tracking Excellent titles. Informal training involves your dog's adaptation to your everyday life. It draws the line between acceptable and unacceptable behavior.

THE RULES OF THE LITTER

Before you even saw your dog, he was being trained by his mother and littermates. From the moment he was born, he had to learn what was acceptable in his animal family. Lines of authority were established: first, the mother, then the most dominating littermate. As a puppy, your dog learned that there were certain things he could and could not do. If he stepped out of line, his mother growled. If he pushed ahead of a certain littermate in the nursing line, he got nipped. By the time your puppy was ready to join a human family, he was aware of such things as limitations and boundaries. The problem with human families, however, is that they often don't know how to communicate their rules, or limitations, clearly to the dog. It really isn't difficult if you give it some thought and try to understand the dog's point of view.

BRINGING A PUPPY HOME

Training begins the moment you pick up the dog. Whether it is good or bad training depends on you. Puppies are too young to be formally trained, but there is a lot you can do to train your new puppy informally by helping him to adapt to your world. Although most people don't realize it, they are training a puppy even when they aren't trying. If you are aware of it, you will make fewer mistakes, and formal training will be easier for you and your dog.

Your puppy probably has never been in a car before, so you are training him when you drive him home. He may not have been in a house before, either. From the time he walks in your front door, he begins to realize what he can and cannot do. That is why it is important for you to be consistent in handling him so that you don't give him conflicting signals. If he knocks over the furniture, chews your favorite shoe or jumps up on the kitchen table and you don't correct him because you plan to start obedience lessons in time, you are training him to do as he pleases. A few weeks later when you start training him to do what pleases you, you will run into problems. If you don't correct the puppy the first time he jumps up on the table, he will think it is permissible to do it. A few weeks later, when you yank him off the table, he will be totally confused.

Correct a puppy with your voice and a firm "No!" You can also use a rolled-up newspaper to hit your hand—not the puppy. The sound will startle him and focus his attention on you. Just don't overdo this kind of correction, because if the puppy becomes accustomed to the sound, he will ignore it. What he needs at this point is a sense of acceptance and inclusion. He won't be ready for formal training until he is six months old, and if you try to rush it, you will depress the dog to the point where learning will be difficult.

He is too young to be given the run of your home. Give him some space of his own, where he knows he won't be disturbed, but let him interact with you and your family so that he begins to feel as if he belongs.

It doesn't make sense to bring a puppy home, put him in a

corner of your kitchen and then go to bed, expecting him to settle down, not to cry and not have to relieve himself before you get up the next morning. A logical approach would be to remind yourself that your puppy has been in a litter, and then ask yourself: How can I make him comfortable in his new surroundings?

He needs to curl up in something warm, because that is what he did among his littermates and with his mother. Warm a few Turkish towels, put them in a box and let your puppy snuggle up in them. Put an alarm clock in among the towels because, to the puppy, the ticking sounds like the beating of his mother's heart. He may not settle down immediately because when he was in a litter he was accustomed to wandering around. But he will settle down more quickly if you use this technique.

Housebreaking your puppy won't take long if you are conscientious about taking him out frequently, and especially after he sleeps, eats or plays. I always advise keeping a puppy in an area with a tile or vinyl floor, such as a bathroom or a portion of the kitchen that can be closed off with a baby gate. This makes cleanup easier when there are accidents—and there *will* be accidents. When they happen, use newspaper to clean up, then take a portion of the soiled newspaper outside to an area where you want your puppy to learn to relieve himself. Weight the paper down with a rock or brick, and always take your puppy out to that area to relieve himself. When he picks up the scent, he will begin to recognize the area. When he uses it properly, make a big fuss over his achievement and give him plenty of praise. Remember to change the piece of paper occasionally.

Your puppy really doesn't want to relieve himself in your house, so all you have to do is work with him. If you will make an effort to know how often your puppy needs to relieve himself, and base your walks outdoors on his natural schedule, you should be able to housebreak him within seven to ten days.

BRINGING AN OLDER DOG HOME

The belief that "you can't teach an old dog new tricks" is absolutely unfounded. If you are reluctant to bring an older dog into your home because you think the dog won't be able to adapt to a new family and environment, relax. The dog will adjust very well if you introduce him properly. There are two steps to this procedure: First you and the dog get acquainted with each other, then you begin your training.

Getting Acquainted

Once you decide to buy or adopt a particular dog that has lived with another family, don't bring the dog home right away. Tell the owners that you want the dog but will take him home in two weeks. Let him stay with his owners during that time, and visit him at least every other day so that you and he can get acquainted in the dog's own territory. This is not the time to train the dog. It is a time to observe him, let him get comfortable with your presence and plan his future training.

Each time you visit, bring an article of your clothing (a sock, a glove, a piece of an old shirt or jeans). Leave it with the dog so he can become familiar with your scent. While the dog is still in his original home, the article doesn't mean much to him, but it is "soaking" him with your scent. When he leaves his original home for your home, that scent will then become an important link between the two homes. He will be bringing something from one into the other, and it will give him a little security.

It is okay for other members of your family to go with you when you visit the dog, as long as there aren't too many at one time. Since you will be meeting the dog on his own territory, he is likely to be protective of it. Depending upon the breed characteristics of the dog, he may feel threatened if several people try to make his acquaintance all at once, especially if they try to do it quickly.

After the first few visits, spend some time alone with the dog, without his owners being present. Take him for a short walk. Play with him and use his favorite toys, which you should arrange to bring with him when you take him home. If he is accustomed to riding in a car, let him sit with you in your car while the motor is running. If he is comfortable doing that, take him for a short ride. By the time you are ready to take the dog home, you will no longer be a stranger and he will be willing to go with you.

Visiting with the dog gives you an opportunity to observe his everyday behavior. You may see some things you will want to change. For instance, he may get up on the furniture, and you may not want him to do that in your home. Don't try to change anything during this time of getting acquainted. The easier you make his transition from one home to another, the easier it will be to retrain him.

Learn as much as you can about the dog from his owners. Begin by asking these questions:

What are the dog's likes and dislikes?
How much training has he had?
Is he housebroken?
Does he ride in a car? Is he comfortable in it?
What does he eat? How much? How often?
What is his medical history?
Which shots has he had? When?
How much exercise does he get? What kind?
How does he behave when he's left alone?
What kind of toys does he like?

You may not get complete answers to your questions. People are sometimes reluctant to admit that they are giving up a dog because it has problems, and they won't want to tell you about them because then you may not want the dog. But realize that owners are more often the cause of a dog's problems, and with proper training you can correct undesirable behavior.

As a condition of purchase, you should have your veterinarian give the dog a complete physical checkup. You will want to know that he has a clean bill of health. You can arrange to take him to your veterinarian after the dog is comfortable in your car. In fact, it is a good reason to go for a short ride.

If, after two weeks' time, you have walked the dog several times, he has been in your car, he has your scent, you have played with each other, you enjoy each other's company and you have some information about his history, you are ready to bring him home with you. When you do that, be sure to arrange to spend some time with him. Don't bring him home on a weekday morning just before you have to go to work, or at night when you are tired and ready to go to bed. Bring him home on a weekend or take some vacation time to be with him. It will be a worthwhile investment in your future friendship, and you will avoid a lot of problems.

Training

Training begins when the dog steps inside your house. This applies to you and any other people in your house as well as to the dog. If the other members of your family have gone with you to visit the dog, he will recognize them. If he is meeting them for the first time, he will be confused and overwhelmed by a welcoming committee, however loving it may be. Prepare the other members of your household ahead of time and tell them not to rush to meet the dog. Tell them to do whatever they would normally do and to ignore the dog. Let him go to them, even if he doesn't do it for a long time. You have to make allowances for the fact that different breeds warm up to people in different ways, so let your dog tell you and your family what is best for him. He will.

A very important thing for everyone in your household to remember is not to reach out and try to pat the dog on the head. This is something people do all the time, and it is something you shouldn't do with any dog, especially when you are meeting a dog for the first time. Most people want to pat a dog on the head to show their affection, but that isn't the way the dog interprets the gesture. The most vulnerable part of a dog's body is the back of the neck—and he knows it. It is the one part of his body he can't defend because he can't reach anything that touches it. In his eyes, a hand coming at him and reaching over his head could be a hand reaching for that indefensible part of his body, and he may react by trying to bite the hand in order to protect himself while he still can.

Instead of reaching out to pat the dog on the head, hold your hand out to him, palm down, and let him sniff it. *Let him touch you first.* Then you can begin to scratch under his chin, rub his neck and work your way up to pat his head, always moving from the front where he can see you. *Never, with any dog, reach in over the dog's head.* You may get away with it if you are lucky, but if you don't and you get bitten, don't blame the dog. He is only following his instincts, and they should be respected. *You made the mistake.*

Use the lead to bring your dog into your house and keep the lead on for a while. The more familiar he is with you, the easier it will be for him to become comfortable in his new home. At this time, don't make demands on him and don't expect him to change his behavior simply because he is in a new environment. He won't be comfortable at first, because he has many adjustments to make. He is coming into contact with new scents, sights and sounds, new people. He is learning about the number of people, their size, their voices and their behavior. His senses need time to process all that information. Sit down and talk to him for a few minutes. When you see that he is curious—and he will be—let him walk around from room to room on the lead. Walk around with him. Ask the other members of your family to behave normally. After the dog has explored the house on a lead, take the lead off and let him walk around on his own. Watch him, but go about your business.

If the dog starts to do something you don't want him to do, such as jumping on a sofa, don't overreact by screaming at him. This is an opportunity to educate him about your rules, and if you alarm him he isn't going to learn anything. Correct him by attaching the lead and snapping it in the manner described in chapter 6, saying "No!" firmly. Get his mind on something else right away by spending a few minutes playing with him. This lets the dog know that even though you didn't like something he did, you still like him.

Don't make the mistake of thinking you should let the dog get settled into your family before you start to train him. That only leads to bad habits that will be much harder for both you and the dog to change. You don't have to train him vigorously at first, but you should certainly let him know what the rules are.

After the dog has had plenty of time to look around your house, put him in a room or an area by himself where he can settle down. Giving him the run of the house as soon as he arrives may seem like a friendly thing to do, but it makes too many demands on the dog. He needs to know that there is one place where he can be left alone and you won't bother him. Give him his old toys and resume your normal home routine. You don't have to isolate the dog; you can put him in a room such as a kitchen or a den where the family members come and go. If you use a baby gate you can confine the dog in a way that allows him to see what's going on around him.

Housebreaking an Older Dog

Be sure to take your dog out often, especially during the first few days when he will be uneasy. If you discover that he was never properly housebroken, don't get upset. That's a problem you can solve, and it may be one that no one took the time to solve earlier in his life. Follow the same procedure you would use for a puppy.

For the first few hours after you bring the dog home, let him roam through the house, first on a lead, then without a lead. But keep your eye on him. After that, it is best to restrict the dog to a room with a tile floor, such as a kitchen or laundry room, so that if there is an accident, the cleanup is easy. I don't advise using a bathroom because it is usually too small.

The older dog won't have to relieve himself as often as a puppy, but it is still important to establish a routine of taking him out at regular intervals. Anytime the dog eats, sleeps or plays, take him outside and let him relieve himself. If the dog relieves himself in the house, say "No!" in a firm, authoritative tone. Don't hit him with a rolled-up newspaper or anything else. Use the newspaper to clean up, and take a portion of the soiled paper outside to an area where you want to dog to learn to relieve himself. Put a rock on top of the paper to keep it in place, and take the dog to the same area each time you take him out. Be patient while he sniffs and investigates. If you stick to a routine and praise the dog enthusiastically every time he relieves himself in the proper place, it shouldn't take him long to catch on to what you want him to do. Until he does, replace the paper occasionally, but not as often as you would for a puppy.

There are a few things to consider before you even try to house-break an older dog. Remember that the dog has to adjust to a new feeding pattern when he moves into another home. Perhaps his former owners didn't feed him at the same time you do, or they may not have fed him at the same time every day. If you are changing the dog's diet, do it gradually or diarrhea and other digestive problems may result. If you seem to be doing everything right and the dog still is relieving himself in the house, take him to your veterinarian. There may be a physical reason for the problem.

Making the Dog Comfortable

Don't decide where the dog should sleep. Let him pick his own spot, provided, of course, that it is not where you don't want him to be, such as in your bed. People may mean well, but they have a way of choosing the worst places for a dog's bedding, such as next to a heater or in a cross-draft between a door and a window. The dog knows better. He is the best judge of what is comfortable and secure. Chances are he won't like fancy commercial beds, so don't waste your money on them. If you brought his bedding from his former home, put it down after he has had an opportunity to find a place that is right for him.

Give your new dog plenty of time to adjust to you, your household members and your way of life. Give yourself time to learn how to look after your dog. Take him for walks, play ball with him, brush his coat and talk to him. Let him know that you are glad to have his company. You can learn a lot about him by observing his behavior, and this is an important foundation for training.

There is no need to confine him after the first few days, because he will begin to realize that your home is his home, too. He will know the members of your household, be familiar with your life-style and be ready to fit in comfortably.

Testing Your Authority

During the time you have been getting familiar with your new dog, he has been evaluating you. Dogs have a keen sense of what people will and won't allow, and your dog will know immediately that your rules aren't the same as the rules in his former home. The most logical way for him to find out what you will and will not allow is to test you. He is trying to find out what his limits are. So if he begins to behave in ways that are different from those you saw when you spent time visiting him, don't get upset. Let him know from the start what his limits are.

For instance, while you are sitting at the table having coffee and doughnuts, the dog may come and sit beside you. Maybe he wasn't fed from the table in his former home, but now he wants to find out if the rules have changed. If you slip him a piece of doughnut, he is going to abandon the old rules and go along with yours. He will be at your side every time you sit down to eat. If this kind of behavior is acceptable to you, you have nothing to worry about. If you don't want to feed the dog from the table, then *don't do it at any time*.

When you take the dog for a walk, he may pull you, even if he never did that before. If you let him do it, the next day he will pull harder. If you correct him the first time he pulls—assuming, of course, that he knows how to walk properly—he will know that there are limits to what he can do. Very quickly he will realize that if he steps outside those limits, he will have a problem, but as long as he stays within those limits, everything will be fine.

The best way for you to let your dog know what the rules are is to give some thought ahead of time to what you will and will not allow. Don't make up the rules after the dog comes into your home for the first time, or as you go along. You will only have to change them, and this will confuse the dog. If you know what you want from the dog, and what you can reasonably expect, you will find it much easier to communicate with him.

THE IMPORTANCE OF EXPOSURE

Your dog has to live in this world, just as you do, and you can help him adapt to it by exposing him to as many different situations as possible. Don't keep him cooped up in a corner of your living room or even in your fenced-in yard. Take him away from his own territory frequently and let him become familiar with new and unfamiliar scents, sights, sounds and behavior. He will be a much more confident dog and you will be a happier owner because you will be able to take him with you more often. The two of you will be partners.

Let Your Dog Explore His World

Remember the first time you boarded a plane or stepped into a boat? Or when you moved from one part of the country to another? Or the first time you did anything new and different? You probably were very nervous. But the second or third time you did it, it was easier because your exposure to the situation helped you overcome your fear of it. This is true of your dog as well. He will be nervous and unsure of himself whenever he is doing something new and different, but by exposing him to normal life situations, you are helping him to learn how to deal with them. With practice and repetition, his anxiety will disappear and he will begin to enjoy doing new things. If you don't allow him to experience new situations while under your control, he will become extremely anxious anytime he has to leave familiar territory and you will find it very difficult to control him.

I always encourage my students to take their dogs into unfamiliar environments, provided, of course, that they do it properly. Otherwise I can predict what is going to happen. After some lessons in basic obedience, the dog appears to be doing well, and the owner is very happy. But eventually the owner takes the dog into a new environment and the dog behaves as if he never heard of the commands. The owner is embarrassed and angry. He takes the dog home and resolves never to take him anywhere again.

A dog, like any other creature with a brain, is curious about the world around him. Encourage him to exercise that curiosity. Let him sniff and investigate. Don't pull him away from leaves, a piece of paper, a stone or a telephone pole just because you are not interested in those things. He is using his intelligence to get information that is useful to him.

If you live in the city, take your dog out into the country when you can and let him experience a different kind of life. If you live in the suburbs, take your dog into the city and let him get used to things like air brakes screeching, people hurrying past the two of you, stopping at traffic lights and crossing busy streets. Sure, it will be difficult in the beginning and your patience will be tested, but if you stay with it, you will be rewarded with a well-adjusted dog that is ready to get up and go anywhere with you the moment you say the word.

Proceed Gradually

The sooner you expose your dog to different environments, the better. This does not mean, however, that you should suddenly thrust your dog into the middle of a new and challenging situation. Give him time to adjust a little at a time. For instance, take him for an occasional walk away from your own neighborhood, even if you have to drive there. Don't get out of your car right away. Leave a door open—better yet, a tailgate, if you drive a station wagon—and just sit there with the dog and let him look around. Talk to him and encourage him, then take him home. Come back in a few days and do the same thing, but this time take the dog out of the car on a lead and have him sit beside you on the sidewalk, where he can get accustomed to people passing by. He will be uncomfortable at first, but if you are patient, he will begin to relax. A few days later you can take him for a short walk, gradually bringing him closer to such things as stores and people.

Shopping centers are wonderful places to expose your dog to new experiences. People are coming and going (some in front of you, some in back), store doors are opening and closing, hot or cold air (depending on the time of year) is coming out of the opening doors, children are racing by on bicycles, cars are going in and out of the parking lot and food scents are drifting out of restaurants. These are things your dog never encounters at home, but wouldn't it be nice to be able to walk him there while you look in the shop windows? If you plan ahead, your dog will adjust after a few visits.

In the beginning follow the same techniques you used when you took your dog for a walk in an unfamiliar neighborhood. Park your car at the far edge of the parking lot where you and your dog can sit and watch the activity from a distance. Go back a few days later and park at the far edge again. This time walk your dog, on a lead, a short distance away from the car and circle around back to the car. Let him sit there beside you, watching, for fifteen or twenty minutes. Talk to him and reassure him. Then take him home. Over several visits, gradually park closer to the store area and walk your dog farther away from the car toward the sidewalk.

Once you get to the sidewalk, people there will react to your dog. Some will avoid him, but some will approach him in all the wrong ways—reaching out to pat him on the head, making strange noises, hugging him and generally confusing him. Avoid problems by telling anyone who wants to approach your dog that you are training him and you have to follow certain rules. Tell them it is okay if they'd like to stand there and talk to you and your dog, but it would be helpful if they didn't try to touch him. If even one person follows your instructions, it will be a very constructive experience for your dog to sit beside you while you talk to someone he doesn't know.

To a dog, one of the most distracting things about a shopping center or a row of stores on a city street are doors that open, suddenly seeming to come straight at him. People come out and go in. Electronically operated doors are especially alarming, because they open unexpectedly. Since you should have your dog on your left side while you are walking with him, start by walking past stores that are on your right side, so that you are closer to the doors than your dog is. He will be startled by the doors at first, but not as much as he would be if you weren't between him and them. Reassure him frequently. Talk to him while you walk. With practice and repetition, you will soon be able to walk him past stores on his side.

PART II

BECOMING EACH OTHER'S BEST FRIEND

Introduction: Step-by-Step Subnovice Lessons (On Lead)

WHENEVER SOMEONE BRINGS me a dog and asks me to train her, I always try to explain that training doesn't work that way. A trainer doesn't train a dog and hand her back to the owner. Good trainers teach both the person and the dog. If I were to train your dog and give her back to you, the training wouldn't hold up, because only one of you would be educated. You wouldn't be able to reinforce my training—you wouldn't know what to do. Your dog would eventually ignore you when you gave a command. If you want a trainer to train your dog, plan to spend some time with the trainer to learn how to handle your dog after she is trained. If you will invest some of your time in doing exactly what the training instructions in this book tell you to do, you can train yourself and your dog very well. Furthermore, since you and your dog can expect to spend many years together, you will continue to learn from each other.

THE BASICS

Subnovice lessons are done with the dog on lead. These exercises form the basic foundation of all obedience training. They are the most important work you and your dog will do. If you don't practice until you can do them perfectly—or as close to perfection as you and your dog can come—the rest of your training will suffer. If you master the basics, the rest of your training will be much easier, because you won't have to keep going back to correct the mistakes you made in the beginning.

But be forewarned. The mechanics of basic obedience exercises can sometimes be boring, monotonous, regimented and disciplined. You will have to do simple things over and over, and you won't do them well for a while because they won't feel natural to you at first. For instance, when you move from a standing position beside your dog (who should be at your *left* side) and you want your dog to move with you, you must always step out on your *left* foot as you give the Heel command. Since that is the foot next to your dog, she can immediately see that you are moving and move accordingly. She keys in on that left foot. When you stop, you must always stop on your left foot and bring your right foot up to your left foot so that your dog will know that you are stopping. Actually you will hesitate almost imperceptibly; neither you nor anyone else will notice it, but your dog will, and your momentary hesitation will be her cue to stop. If you want your dog to stay in place while you walk away, you must step out on your *right* foot as you give the Stay command and/or the hand signal, because that foot, being farther away, tells her that you don't want her to move with you. Up until now, you probably never gave a thought to which foot you used when taking a first step, so expect to feel awkward until you do it so many times that it becomes second nature. Most of my students become so accustomed to stepping out on their left foot that they do it wherever they are, with or without their dog.

Probably neither you nor your dog will enjoy all your basic obedience lessons, but if you want to go on to the rewarding parts of training—and there are many—it is worth your time and effort to do them conscientiously and regularly. You won't always be in the mood to work with your dog. You may be pressed for time. The weather may be unpleasant—or it may be so pleasant that you would

Placing the dog in the Sit position

rather do something else. Your dog won't like the repetition and regimentation any more than you do and will be happy to skip a lesson. The temptations will be many, but I advise you not to give in to them. As frustrating as the early stages of training may sometimes be, you will—if you persist and follow the instructions carefully—reach that moment when you and your dog work as one. I have had students who even remember the exact time of the exact day when it happened. It is that rewarding. And from there on it just gets better.

A POSITIVE ATTITUDE

Each time you work with your dog, try to end your lesson on a positive note. That is not as easy as you might think, because there will be days when nothing seems to go right for you or your dog. These are the times when you really have to demonstrate your commitment. If neither you nor your dog are in the mood to practice, and if you are both doing everything wrong, that is *not* the time to cut the lesson short. If you do, your frustration will carry over into your next lesson and you won't do any better. If you are having difficulty, stay with the exercise until you do it properly—maybe not brilliantly, but properly. Then, before you quit, give your dog a command you know you both can execute well—and praise her lavishly for doing it. Spend a little time playing with your dog. Your feeling of accomplishment will carry over into your next lesson, and you will both work much better.

Ending a lesson on a positive note is especially important during Subnovice training, where the frustrations are many and the gratification is delayed. If you've had a particularly trying lesson one day, begin your next lesson the same way you ended the previous one: with a command you and the dog can execute well. Build up gradually to the more difficult exercises, and then end on another positive note. This will do as much for your ego as it will for your dog's.

Building handler confidence:
the lead over the shoulder

A fundamental step in the Recall

YOU ARE THE TEACHER

Subnovice lessons are the very beginning of formal obedience training. Your goal is to gain control over the dog, so your hands will often be on the dog as you go through the exercises. For example, you will notice that when your dog is on her own, she may choose to sit down at any old time of day, but that is not the same as knowing how to sit on command. Don't assume that when you say "Sit," she is going to know what you mean by it. You will have to teach the dog by moving her into a Sit position physically, but in a manner that communicates to her what she must eventually do for herself. If you take a shortcut and push the dog into a Sit position, you aren't teaching her anything because you haven't shown her how to use her body. You have to put her in a Sit position, moving her muscles and body in a way she can duplicate for herself. Then the mechanics will make sense to her. The same is true for all the basic exercises.

Subnovice is much like kindergarten; you have to lead your dog through each exercise. This is why you need the lead. If you take the lead off at this point, you will lose control of your dog. All the work in Subnovice is done with the dog on lead, with you showing your dog, in detail, how each exercise is to be done. The catch is that you don't know how to do the exercises either, so you have to learn along with your dog. Expect to feel awkward. Everybody does. At first you and your dog will stumble through the exercises, but with repetition you both will get much better.

Remember that your dog learns how to do each exercise by keying in on what you do with your body. If you don't learn how to do your part of an exercise properly, you won't be able to teach your dog how to do her part. This is why it is important for you to spend some time practicing the exercises *without* your dog before you try to do them with your dog.

None of these exercises is difficult, but because they will be new to you they have to be broken down into steps that you can master one at a time. The hand and foot movements won't seem natural to you at first, so it will be less confusing to your dog if you work on them alone until you can do them with some degree of ease. Then you can pay attention to what your dog is doing and help her to learn the proper moves.

Expect to make mistakes, whether working alone or with your

The attentive look

dog. You can learn a lot from them. To my way of thinking, mistakes are steps toward perfection because they make you aware of your weak points. Once you know what they are, you can work on strengthening them.

MAINTAINING ENTHUSIASM

Although I have already stated that you should aim at perfection, I mean that in terms of long-range goals. *When it comes to learning basic Subnovice exercises, I don't advise practicing each one until you reach perfection before going on to the next lesson.* If you do that, you and your dog will get so bored that you will find it hard to learn anything. Instead, *combine new exercises with a review of previous ones.*

A sensible training schedule, in terms of the time it should take to learn each lesson, is as follows:

Heel, About-Turn, Sit	one week
Corners, Automatic Sit	one week
Sit-Stay	one week
Figure Eight, Stand	one week
Down	one week
Recall	two weeks

If you have spent a week learning the Heel, About-Turn and Sit, but you and your dog are far from perfect, go on to Corners and the Automatic Sit. But begin your training session by going through the Heel, About-Turn and Sit before you start the new exercises. If you make a point of reviewing all your previous exercises before doing a new one, you will notice a definite improvement in your performance. In fact, review should always be part of your training sessions, no matter how well you are doing. It will keep you sharp.

Plan to work an hour each day with your dog. If you prefer, you can break that down into two half-hour sessions, or even three twenty-minute sessions. Keep close track of the time you spend training. You will be tempted to stop a few minutes earlier on some occasions, but if you do that, it will become a habit. Soon you will be working only a few minutes a day, and that simply isn't enough. Eventually, when your dog is trained, you can work with her a few times a week, perhaps for only twenty minutes at a time. But you are

64

Relaxing after a training session

not anywhere near that point now. It is something to work toward.

By the end of the Subnovice lessons, you and your dog should be able to execute all the basic exercises on command, at least close to perfection, *without the aid of the lead.* Of course, you will still be using the lead, but it will function as a safety factor. You will be ready to move on to Novice lessons.

6

The Proper Equipment and How to Use It

Always buy good equipment—it will work with you instead of against you while you are training your dog. It will also save you the cost of replacing inferior equipment that doesn't hold up.

THE LEAD

The lead is an instrument of control, a means of communication, a safety device and an aid in training your dog. Put some thought into choosing one.

I prefer a quality leather lead for several reasons. It is strong, flexible and comfortable. A nylon or webbing lead is hard to hold. It can slip through your hands and burn them during some of the more strenuous exercises, or at any time if your dog is big, untrained and able to pull you around. I don't allow chain leads in my classes because they are heavy and uncomfortable to hold. They may also cause injuries. If you or your dog get tangled up in a chain lead, you both might get hurt.

Clockwise, from top left: flat leather collar, common choker chain, combination leather and chain collar, standard 6-foot leather lead, intermediate lead, grab lead.

A leather lead should be five or six feet long. It will stretch some with use. A lead that is both stitched and riveted will be stronger. Stay away from skinny leads in pretty colors because they will break if your dog makes one good lunge after something he would like to chase. Insist on good, substantial leather and take care of it by rubbing it with neats-foot oil about once a month. While the price will be higher than that of other leads initially, you will have it for years. If the stitching or rivets wear out, you can take the lead to your local shoemaker for repairs.

The only time to buy a cheap lead is when you are introducing a puppy to a lead. This should be done before you are ready to take the dog out for a walk, and its primary purpose is to acquaint the dog with the lead. To you, a lead may make perfect sense, but to a puppy it can be frightening to have something long and unfamiliar trailing from her neck. Acquaint her gradually and for short periods of time, and practice only when you are with the dog all the time. Never leave a collar or a lead on an unattended dog, because it can get caught in furniture; when the puppy tries to free herself she can get hurt.

Holding the Lead

How you hold the lead is very important. If you make the mistake of wrapping it around your hand, which many untrained people do, you will be in trouble if the dog pulls because you won't be able to free your hand. Even a leather lead, if pulled tight, can break some of the small bones in your hand.

Do not put your entire hand through the loop and hold onto the flat part of the lead. One good tug from your dog and your hand will open and the loop will slip off.

Do not put four fingers through the loop and clench the lead. If your dog pulls the lead hard, the pressure will cause your hand to open and the loop will slip free.

Here is the best and simplest way to hold a lead comfortably and securely:

Hold the lead, loop end up, in your left hand.
Extend your right hand, fingers flat and together, thumb at a right angle to your fingers, as if you were going to shake someone's hand.

Put your right thumb—*only your right thumb*—through the loop of the lead, and let the lead hang down against your right palm.

Close the fingers of your right hand around the part of the loop that rests in the palm of your hand.

Run your left hand down the lead toward the clip end that will be fastened to the dog's collar and gather up the slack in the lead, allowing it to bow loosely in front of your knees.

You will find that even if you are pulled off balance, your hand will instinctively close around the loop in your hand because your thumb has closed down on it and is holding it fast. You can close your fingers around the lead firmly, yet you won't suffer any pain or damage to your hand.

Using the Lead

The loop end of the lead should always be held in your right hand, even if you are left-handed (as I am). Your dog should be on your left side. Use your left hand to control the slack in the lead and to make corrections by snapping it (see chapter 7).

You don't use a lead to *make* your dog do an exercise, you use the lead to *teach* your dog how to do an exercise. How you guide her through the various steps has to make sense to her, just as your part in the exercise has to make sense to you.

Your aim in using the lead is to take your dog through the basic exercises without pulling it taut. Of course, you won't be able to do this in the beginning, but eventually you should be able to execute all the commands with a slack lead. By the time you accomplish this, your dog will be responding to your verbal commands because she will already know what she is supposed to do with her body. At first, however, you will use the lead to demonstrate to your dog what you want her to do when you give a command. How you handle it is even more important than what your dog does at the other end, because if you use it uncertainly, she will know it sooner than you do. As I have mentioned, your dog is extremely sensitive to your body's action. For instance, if your dog performs incorrectly and you hesitate to snap the lead and release it, your dog will sense that hesitation and know that you aren't confident about correcting her. She won't be sure what you want her to do, because your body action tells her that you aren't sure. If you fidget with the lead and run your left hand up and down as you walk, you are telling your dog that you are about to do something—such as turn around, go in another direction or stop. When you don't do any of those things, but instead keep walking, you confuse your dog.

Any time you pick up your lead and attach it to your dog's collar, remember that it is a sensitive communication system between the two of you. Always be aware of how you are handling it, so that you don't send the wrong messages to your dog.

The Intermediate Lead

When you work your way up to doing the Recall with your dog, you will need a long lead that allows you to walk some distance away while your dog is in the Sit position. For this exercise, and for some later ones, you should use a twenty-five-foot intermediate lead.

I don't recommend buying a leather intermediate lead because it would be very expensive (if you could even find one), and you won't be using it often enough to justify the expense. You can do very well using a webbed lead. You won't have to worry about hurting your hands, because you won't be using this lead in the same way as you use your standard leather lead. Also, by the time you need the intermediate lead, your dog should be well past the stage where she is likely to pull you around.

Because this lead is so long, it can easily get tangled. Be sure to wind it neatly around your arm after each use, so that when you want it, you won't have to unravel it.

THE COLLAR

Before you choose a collar for your dog, consider three things: good quality, the right fit and proper use. Ignoring any one of these factors can affect your training and cause your dog discomfort.

You can use a flat or rolled leather collar for your dog if you prefer, but only when you aren't using the lead or training your dog. A flat collar, or even a rolled one, provides very little control over your dog because you can't tighten and quickly release it. All you can do is pull—and your dog, of course, will pull in the opposite direction.

I prefer to work with a choker chain. Some people think a choker chain is cruel, but I can assure you it isn't and never was meant to be. It is not designed, and should never be used, to hurt the dog. It is designed, and should be used, to gain the dog's attention by closing briefly around the dog's neck muscles on either side of the windpipe when the owner snaps the lead quickly and immediately releases it. The pressure is distributed around the dog's neck rather than on the windpipe.

A choker chain—or any collar, for that matter—can be harmful if it is put on the dog incorrectly or if the owner handles it incorrectly. That is true of a lead as well. But if the choker chain is the proper size, and if it is both put on the dog and handled correctly by the owner, the result is simply good training.

Be sure to buy the correct size. If your chain is too big you won't be able to make corrections quickly, because it will take too long for the chain to snap into position and release. A choker chain of the correct size should just slip over the dog's head. Remember, it is a collar, not a necklace. If the collar slides down to the broader part of the neck, where the muscles are thicker, you won't be able to snap it quickly and precisely to get the dog's attention. If you think of the chain as a signal, it will help you to choose the correct size and handle it properly.

How to Put the Chain on Your Dog

I've known students to come back, lesson after lesson, with the dog's collar on backwards. Putting it on properly is really quite simple, but you have to pay attention to the details until they become automatic.

1. The chain has a ring at each end. Hold one ring in your left hand and one in your right hand.
2. Bring your left hand up over your right hand until the chain is taut and the two rings are in line with each other, one over the other.
3. Lower your left hand, letting the chain slide through the ring at the bottom (in your right hand) until the two rings meet. The chain has now become a circle connected by the two rings. One ring (the one that was in your left hand) pulls the chain through the other.

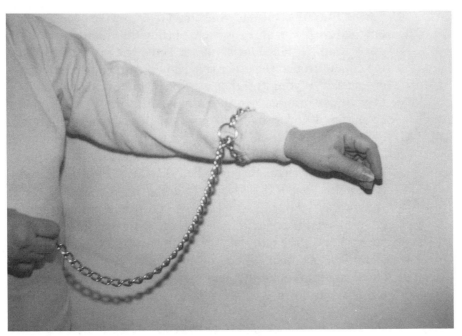

The wrong way to put the collar on

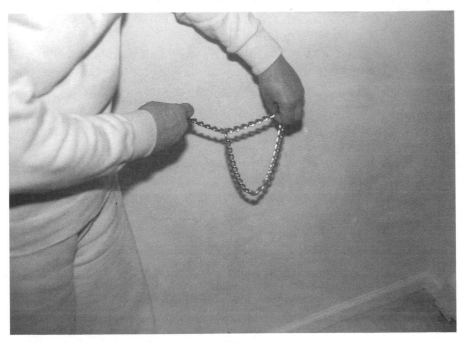

The right way

4. Spread the circle and slide the chain over your left hand and onto your left arm as if you were putting the chain over your dog's head. If the collar is on correctly, the ring that pulls the chain through the other ring should come down, not up, on the side of your arm that is next to your body (right side of your left arm). Correspondingly, the ring would come around and down the dog's neck on the side next to your body (the right side of her neck), not up from under her chin.
5. Test the collar on your arm by attaching the lead to the ring that pulls the chain through the other ring. Pull the chain taut and release it quickly. If the collar is on correctly, the chain should tighten and release smoothly and immediately.
6. If you have the collar on backwards, with the pulling ring coming down the outer side of your arm (the left side), the chain will get stuck when you pull on it. You will see the chain coming from underneath your arm rather than across the top and down the side next to your body.

As complicated as this may seem when you first put the collar on your arm, it will be easy after you try it a few times. Check the photographs carefully as you practice. Don't put the collar on your dog until you can do it comfortably and know you are doing it correctly, or you will confuse your dog.

If the collar isn't put on properly, you won't be able to use your lead well, and your dog will be uncomfortable. So check the collar every time you put it on your dog. I still do.

The Puppy's Collar

If you just brought a puppy home, you will need to use a collar to take her out for a walk and to relieve herself. *Don't use a choker chain yet. Wait until you are ready to begin training.* Puppies are so active that they can easily get caught in a choker collar and might get hurt trying to pull free. Use a flat, not rolled, collar at this time, and do not leave the puppy alone while she is wearing the collar. Always be with her or at least have her in sight.

It will take time for your puppy to feel comfortable in a collar, and it should be introduced gradually. Put it on briefly while you are playing with her. Then take the collar off. Put it on and take if off a few times. Do this for several days, leaving the collar on for longer periods of time, until the puppy begins to forget she is wearing it. Then you can attach a lightweight lead and allow the puppy to walk around your house trailing the lead after her. Don't leave it on for long. Take it off and continue playing. After a while your puppy will be at ease with the collar and lead and your early training will be much more enjoyable. The reason I advise buying a cheap lead at this point is that, no matter how closely you watch the puppy, she may start chewing on the lead simply because it is there and she is a puppy.

Usually, when people buy a collar for a puppy, they buy one that's too big for the dog because they assume the dog will grow into it. In the meantime, the poor little puppy keeps tripping over the collar because it hangs down to the ground. It is better to accept the fact that you will go through several collars while your puppy is growing and buy the correct size every time. A dog should always feel comfortable in a collar.

7
Establishing Authority

PEOPLE SOMETIMES ASSUME that training is a matter of asking their dog to perform certain feats. They think their dog will do anything for them out of love and devotion. That simply isn't true. If you haven't taught your dog how to do what you want her to do, she won't be able to execute a command no matter how much she loves you. And unless you establish yourself as the authority in your dog's life, you won't be an effective teacher. Loving you won't make your dog willing to do what she doesn't want to do—and the work involved in the early stages of training is not what she wants to do. Neither do you. In order to achieve your goal of being good companions, the two of you will have to overcome your dislike of rules, regimentation and repetition. You will have to do it first because you are the one who has to make the rules.

Don't be put off by the word "authority." It doesn't mean that you treat your dog shabbily or are insensitive to her needs. On the contrary, having authority over your dog means that you know what she needs and how to take good care of her. It means you take responsibility for teaching her how to live in your world. Your dog depends upon you and your authority, so it is important to let her know that you are there for her. It is part of the animal-god relationship.

In the Subnovice lessons, along with the mechanics of executing each command, you will learn how to develop your authority and communicate it to your dog.

THE COMMANDS

Keep your words to a minimum when giving commands. When you are talking to your dog informally, you can speak in any way you choose, but when you are giving a command, keep it simple. Why clutter up your dog's memory bank with unnecessary words? Instead of teaching your dog to come to you by saying "King, come over here," just say "King, come." Don't say "Sit down," say "Sit." In fact, if you say "Sit down," you are giving your dog two different commands, "Sit" and "Down." If you are speaking informally and simply want your dog to settle down, say something like "Go lie down" to distinguish it from the command "Down." "Go lie down" is a request, not a command. It means your dog is free to choose a comfortable place to lie down. But if you want to give your dog a command to stop in her tracks and drop to the ground, use only "Down," and say it with authority.

Don't give a command and keep repeating it if your dog ignores you. When you give a formal command, say the word once. If your dog doesn't obey the command, make a correction and give the command again. Do this until your dog carries out the command properly. When she does, praise her for it, no matter how many times she did it wrong.

THE VALUE OF PRAISE AND CORRECTION

The three basic elements of training are praise, correction and consistency in praising and correcting.

Put yourself in the dog's place. Suppose you were working at jumping over a hurdle on command. If the person teaching you were to say "Hey, that's great!" every time you did it correctly—or even every time you did it just a little bit better—you'd be eager to do it again. If your teacher didn't praise you, would you want to keep trying? If your teacher constantly criticized your performance and told you everything you did was wrong, would you even want to go

Praising enthusiastically

near a hurdle? If you kept getting rejected, wouldn't you be discouraged?

In the beginning of your training, encourage your dog by praising her when she shows some improvement, not only when she does something correctly. This will make her want to do better next time.

Don't be inconsistent when you praise or correct your dog. Always remember to praise her convincingly, and always take time to correct her. Inconsistency in praising and correcting is unfair to the dog. Consider the dog whose owner praises her performance one minute and ignores it the next. Or the owner who corrects a dog for disobeying and then lets her get away with it another time. If someone treated you that way, would you know what the rules are? Inconsistency in praise and correction can undermine hours of diligent practice, because you are giving mixed signals to your dog. Don't praise your dog extravagantly when you are having a good day and ignore her accomplishments when you are feeling down. Give her praise based upon *her performance*, not upon your moods. Similarly, don't be uneven in your corrections. Correct her immediately every time she does something wrong; don't make excuses for her just because you are too tired to repeat the exercise until she gets it right.

Praise is your most valuable teaching aid if you give it with enthusiasm. A simple, mild-mannered "Good girl" won't do. Put some feeling into it, no matter how many times you praise your dog. Pat her shoulder in appreciation. I don't advise physical forms of praise while the dog is executing an exercise. Praise her verbally to encourage her. Pat her and praise her physically when she finishes the exercise. Praise is especially important in the early training lessons when both you and your dog are struggling against frustration. You'll feel good giving the praise and your dog will feel wonderful getting it.

YOUR ATTITUDE

Your attitude influences the effectiveness of your training. Don't pretend to be someone else. Don't imitate a trainer or a friend who seems to know how to handle a dog. Be yourself, but always remain conscious of your actions. Even though you have to pay attention to what your dog is doing, watch what you are doing, too.

Know whether you are doing something right or wrong. If you are giving your dog the wrong signals and don't realize it, your dog can't possibly realize it, either. She can't perform any better than you can. If you are doing something wrong, correct it. Don't blame your dog. When you know you are doing something right, you will have confidence giving a command, and it will travel straight down the lead to your dog.

Eventually, as you master the basics of training, your actions will become automatic and you won't have to pay as much attention to each step. Without even thinking about it, both you and your dog will make the right moves.

YOUR TONE OF VOICE

How do you sound when you give your dog a command? If you drawl a mild "Lady, come," she will drift toward you as if she's got all the time in the world. If you shout, she may not move at all, or she may run the other way. Authority doesn't have to be loud. Say a brisk, firm "Lady, come!" and she will move faster.

One day when you are about to work with your dog, put a tape recorder in your pocket and let it run. Play the tape back when you are finished. You will be amazed at what you hear. If you are like most people, you will speak in many different ways during the lesson, and you will be able to recognize the advantages of firm commands.

Dogs respond better to deeper voices, because they sound more authoritative. If your voice is high, or if it gets high when you are under stress, concentrate on developing a slightly lower tone of voice when working with your dog.

USING THE LEAD TO CORRECT

"No" is the only word you will need to correct your dog. Say it sharply and reinforce its meaning by snapping the lead, which instantly tightens and then releases the choker collar. Eventually you will be able to correct the dog verbally in most instances.

I often find that people are reluctant to snap the lead because they think the collar action hurts the dog. Let me assure you that it doesn't. If the collar is on correctly and you snap the lead properly, you will get your dog's attention and communicate the fact that she did something wrong. If you don't snap the lead, your dog may ignore your commands because she knows that you aren't going to insist that she obey them.

Snapping the lead demonstrates your control over your dog at this point in your training. If you were to try to correct your dog by pulling her, it would become a test of strength. A large dog will win, while a small dog will simply be intimidated rather than instructed. But by snapping the lead properly, you can get a St. Bernard up onto his feet when he has no intention of moving. It is a matter of dexterity rather than strength. Naturally, if you are working with a Cocker Spaniel you should snap the lead with less force than you would with a Great Dane. What you are communicating to your dog, once he understands the command, is: Do it right—it is easier that way.

In the early part of your training, you may have to snap the lead several times, in rapid succession, to make your correction. How many times will depend upon the size of your dog, her breed and her individual characteristics. The way you snap the lead will also vary according to what your dog is doing. For instance, she may be pulling away from you and the lead is taut, or she may be stationary and the lead is bowed.

To correct effectively, you will have to learn to snap the lead properly. In the beginning you should work without your dog until you can snap the lead smoothly. Assume that the lead is attached to your dog and you are holding the loop end in your right hand.

If the lead is taut and your dog is pulling away from you:

Step 1: With both hands on the lead, move the lead a few inches *toward* your dog until it is slack or bowed.

Step 2: Quickly and firmly jerk your hands back toward your body and away from your dog, drawing the lead taut. This will activate the choker collar and bring your dog's attention back to you. Do this very quickly. At the same time that you jerk the lead, say "No!"

Step 3: Move your hand forward again, *toward* the dog, to loosen the choker collar. This three-part action—*toward the dog, away from the dog, toward the dog*—should take no more than a fraction of a second.

Step 4: Immediately repeat the command. If your dog doesn't obey, snap the lead again as you say "No!" and repeat the command again. *Command, correct, command* as many times as necessary until your dog obeys.

Step 5: When your dog executes the command correctly, praise her vigorously.

Review. The snapping motions are: both hands on the lead, toward the dog, then away from the dog as you say "No!" then back toward the dog—as fast as you can do it. You will hear and feel the chain sliding smoothly if you are doing it correctly. You will hear and feel it snag if you are doing it incorrectly—if that happens, correct your own mistake immediately by loosening the dog's collar. *Check to see that you have the collar on properly.*

If the lead is bowed because your dog is close to you and will not move on command:

Step 1: Holding the loop end of the lead in your right hand, take up the slack in the lead by grasping it with your left hand and pulling it toward you.

Step 2: Move the lead toward your dog, as in step 1 above.

Step 3: Jerk the lead away from your dog, as in step 2 above, and say "No!"

Step 4: Immediately move the lead *toward* your dog, as in step 3 above.

Step 5: Finish with steps 4 and 5 above.

As you proceed through the Subnovice lessons you will learn other variations of snapping the lead, depending upon your dog's position, her distance from you and the exercise. Most of the time, however, you will use the basic techniques described above.

Snapping the lead is easy, but it will take some practice before you can do it smoothly. Don't practice on your dog. Use a fencepost, a log sunk into the ground or any other kind of pole (such as the ones you often find in playgrounds). If you become proficient in snapping the lead before you try it on your dog, you won't have to do it as often to make your point.

CORRECTION AS COMMUNICATION

Correcting your dog is tricky business. If you overcorrect, you can break a dog's spirit and ruin her by making her too depressed to learn anything. If you undercorrect, you are actually teaching the dog to disobey you. Most people undercorrect, usually because they don't understand what correction means. They think of it as punishment.

I like to think of correction as a form of communication. It tells the dog that you are displeased with what she did, that you expect her to carry out your commands and will accept nothing less. However, before you can ask your dog to carry out a command, you have to be sure that you have taught her what the command means.

If your dog understands what you want her to do when you give a specific command and she doesn't execute it properly, snap the lead and say "No" firmly. Immediately repeat the command. If you don't get an obedient response from the dog, repeat the correction and repeat the command. Correct the dog as many times as it takes for her to realize that obedience is the easy way out.

The four steps of correction are *command, correction, command, praise.* Never omit one of them, especially that second command and the praise.

Be Honest About Your Anger

If you are angry, let the dog know it—but only if your anger is under control. Don't walk away from the dog or postpone training until you are calmer. Make the correction while you are still hot under the collar. Let your voice express your feelings, but make the correction properly. Training can be very frustrating at times, and the person who doesn't ever get angry—with himself and with the dog—may not really be putting much effort into his work.

In my classes I often come across a dog owner who absolutely refuses to snap the lead and speak sharply to his dog. "I wouldn't do that to my children," he'll say to me, "so why should I do it to my dog?" I tell him that I can't vouch for the behavior of his children, but I can assure him that if his dog isn't corrected when she disobeys, she will continue disobeying. Eventually the person who doesn't want to correct his dog gets to the point where he is furious because nothing is going right. As he sees it, the dog is stupid, he is stupid, the lead is stupid, the collar is stupid and it is a rotten day! Finally, on his own and because he is so frustrated, he will do what I have been telling him to do for weeks: With a genuine tone of authority in his voice, he will snap the lead, command the dog into a particular position and the dog will obey—not only instantly but eagerly. From then on, training becomes satisfying rather than frustrating for both the dog and owner.

Of course, if you can't control your anger, by all means stop working with your dog. Wait a few days and start your training over again. But work on controlling your anger as part of your own training.

Put Some Praise into Your Correction

After every correction, it is important to show your dog some affection so that she knows you still care for her. But don't do it too quickly. Wait a little while. Then give her a command you know she will execute well, and praise her generously. Pick up a toy and play with her. If you do this, your corrections will reinforce the rules you have already taught your dog and won't damage your relationship.

8

Heel, About-Turn

Learning Time: One week

IN MY CLASSES I teach the Heel and About-Turn exercises as a unit. Although each exercise is broken down into steps that have to be learned separately, both are so closely related that it makes sense to work on them simultaneously.

HEEL

Practical Application

I'm often asked, "Why does my dog have to heel? Why can't he just walk?" Walking your dog in the heel position allows both you and your dog the maximum amount of freedom of movement while your dog is under your control. You can make any type of movement, go in any direction or stop entirely and your dog will pick up the cue immediately and move with you.

If the dog were to walk ahead of you, he wouldn't be able to coordinate his actions quickly enough to move with you. If you were to turn suddenly to the left, you might trip over the dog. If you turned to your right, your dog would have to catch up with you. If the dog were to walk even slightly behind you, he would miss most of your cues.

When your dog is trained, there will be times when you will want to walk with him informally, without commands. But you will have the assurance that you can command him to heel at your side at any time.

The Mechanics

When you begin this exercise, your dog doesn't have to be sitting at your side (unless you commanded him to be there), but when you move, he should move with you. When you stop, he should stop beside you, with his front legs parallel to your left leg. He should not walk close enough to be touching you, but there should be very little daylight between you. The reason for heeling your dog on your left side is that, historically, dogs were handled primarily by men, and men always walked on the street side of the path or sidewalk when they accompanied women. Keeping the dog on the man's left side allowed the dog more space to move and a better opportunity to see what was coming toward him. Times have changed, but the tradition lives on.

Before you give the Heel command, call your dog's name; this focuses his attention on you. The Heel and the Recall are the only two basic exercises that require you to call your dog's name before giving him the command. Both these exercises get the dog moving; the others—Sit, Stay, Down—are done with the dog in place. Consequently, after a little practice, the dog will hear his name and be alert for a command to move.

Always hesitate after you say your dog's name, and before giving the Heel command. Eventually, in the Recall, you will use this procedure again. If he moves on the name and before you give the command, correct him and repeat the command, beginning with his name. Expect this sort of thing to happen, because your dog quickly realizes that a certain command will follow his name. He will take a shortcut by executing the command before you give it. When you correct him for starting too soon, you are telling him, "You don't give the commands—I do." This reinforces your authority.

To begin the Heel exercise, place the loop end of the lead in your right hand, with your thumb through the loop. Your left hand

Proper Heel position

Dog stays close in About-Turn

takes up the slack in the lead. *Do not take up so much slack that the lead is taut. It should bow slightly.*

With your dog sitting on your left side, say his name, hesitate and give the command "Heel" as you move forward on your *left* foot. If your dog doesn't move with you, *do not repeat the command.* Snap the lead, say "No!" and then repeat the command. The lead, from the dog's collar to your left hand, should be slightly bowed as you walk together. Eventually, when you take your left hand off the lead, the lead should be slightly bowed across the front of your legs.

In the beginning, your dog will do everything wrong. Remember that you know what you want him to do, but he doesn't. For now, the word "Heel" means nothing to him. Repetition and correction will give it meaning. Until that happens, you will need to be patient. You have much to learn, but your dog has more because he doesn't speak your language. Give him time to read your actions. Encourage him by praising him for the smallest improvement.

Your dog will most likely make one or more of the following mistakes:

> forge—he is getting ahead of you
> lag—he is falling behind you
> heel wide—he is parallel to your left leg, but he is too far out
>   to the left
> crowd—he is pushing against your left leg

Use the lead and the snapping action to make corrections for these heeling mistakes, but correct in the direction opposite to the dog's movement.

Forging. To bring your dog back in line with your left leg, use your left hand to take up the slack and snap the lead straight back. Call your dog's name, say "No" and repeat the command "Heel." As soon as your dog begins to do it right, praise him enthusiastically.

Lagging. Snap the lead forward as you say "No." Call your dog's name, repeat "Heel." Then praise verbally.

Lagging sometimes indicates extreme shyness or lack of confidence in a dog, so before making a correction you should attempt to determine whether your dog is lagging because he is stubborn or because he has a problem. If he seems to be shy, coax him forward instead of snapping the lead, and you will increase his confidence. If you determine that your dog lags because he is stubborn and doesn't want to obey your command, snap the lead to bring him forward.

Dog stays close in About-Turn

Resuming Heel after About-Turn

91

Heeling wide. Bring your right hand (still holding the loop end) across to your left hand; using both hands, snap the lead toward your right, say "No" and repeat "Heel." Praise.

Crowding. This is the only time you should not use the lead to correct a mistake. Instead, bump your dog with your left knee as you say "No" and repeat "Heel." *For small dogs, brush the* side *of your shoe—never the toe—against him.* Praise.

Corrections and Praise

There are three steps in a correction: command, correction, command. Timing the correction is very important, and it will take a while before you do it well. If your dog executes the command correctly, don't snap the lead at all. Praise him verbally. But if he doesn't immediately execute the command correctly, snap the lead and make the correction. What you want to avoid is getting into a habit of snapping the lead without giving your dog a chance to do the exercise correctly. If you are correcting him before he does something wrong, you are not teaching him anything. Daily practice with your dog is the best way I know to develop good timing.

If you are quick to encourage your dog by praising him, these early mistakes will not become problems. Use verbal praise while you are doing the exercises and save the physical praise until the lesson is finished. Physical praise, such as patting his shoulder or rubbing his coat, will interfere with his concentration. Verbal praise gets across the message that your dog is doing something correctly without leading him to think that the lesson is over.

Your attitude and tone of voice mean more than your words. At the end of each lesson, say "Okay!" enthusiastically, as if to say, "School is out!" This lets your dog know that he is no longer on command and can do as he pleases. Encourage him to look forward to these times by playing with him after the lessons. The next day, play with him again before you begin another lesson.

The Checklist

In the beginning of training, you won't always know when you are making a mistake because you will be so busy watching what your dog is doing. A checklist will help to focus your attention on your own actions, but only if you use it properly. Don't make excuses for yourself or your dog. If one or both of you is making a mistake, work on correcting it. If your dog is heeling a few inches ahead or behind, that is not good enough. If you aren't handling the lead smoothly, spend more time practicing without your dog. It is only when mistakes are ignored that they turn into problems. Use the checklist at the end of each lesson to evaluate your progress. When you and your dog are heeling:

- Where is your dog's head?
  Is it out in front of your left leg?
  Is it behind?
  Is it touching you?
  Can you get more than the width of your hand between you and your dog?
- Is your dog jumping up at the lead?
- Are you holding the lead properly? Are you putting your right thumb through the loop, taking up the slack with your left hand, closing your four fingers and dropping your thumb over the lead, trapping it in your right hand? Your left hand should then move down the lead, taking up the excess slack, leaving the lead slightly bowed as you heel.
- Are you stepping off on your left foot?
  Do you give the command "Heel" as you step off?
- Are you giving commands with authority and praise with enthusiasm?
- Are you making the proper corrections?
  Are you remembering to command-correct-command when your dog makes a mistake?
  Are you snapping the lead in the opposite direction when your dog forges, lags or heels widely?
  Are you using your left knee or your left foot to "bump" your dog when he crowds?

ABOUT-TURN

Practical Application

The simplest way for me to explain the reason for the About-Turn is to ask you, "Did you ever change your mind?" When you are heeling your dog, you may decide to turn around and go in the opposite direction. Actually, you don't even have to change your mind. You may finish your walk at a certain point and turn around to go home. Teaching your dog the About-Turn enables him to coordinate his movement to your change of direction without getting confused or tangled in the lead.

The About-Turn also tells your dog to pay attention to you; otherwise you may be alongside him one moment and gone the next.

The Mechanics

The About-Turn is always made by turning to your right and going in the opposite direction. Later on, you can About-Turn to your left, if you choose, but it involves switching the lead from one hand to another, and at this point I don't advise trying it.

Give the Heel command and move forward with your dog. When you are ready to turn around and go in the opposite direction, as your left foot hits the ground, pivot on the balls of both feet simultaneously, 180 degrees to your right, keeping your hands down, and step out immediately on your left foot. Repeat the Heel command as you do this. After a week of practicing the About-Turn, you can stop repeating "Heel" as you make your turn. By that time, your dog will be following your movement and should not need the command repeated. Be sure to keep your hands down as you pivot. If you raise them, you will pull your dog into you as you turn.

Do this exercise quickly. In the beginning your dog probably won't follow your body as you turn. He may not even be looking at you. But suddenly you won't be there beside him. Snapping the lead will tell him to stay in line with your leg even when you move in another direction.

Your dog's head should stay in line with your left leg as you make your 180-degree turn. The instant he isn't in line, snap the lead, say "No" and repeat the Heel command. Remember to keep your hands down when you snap the lead in the About-Turn. At first, you will do what many people do: You will raise your hands as you snap the lead, and that tells the dog to sit. Practice without your dog until you can turn and snap the lead quickly without raising your hands.

Your dog will make the same four mistakes of forging, lagging, heeling wide and crowding when you do the About-Turn. Correct him by snapping the lead in the opposite direction and using your knee or shoe when he crowds.

The Checklist

- Are you pivoting on both feet and stepping out on your left foot as you move in the opposite direction?
- Are you making the turn quickly?
- Does your dog's head stay in line with your left leg when you make your About-Turn?
- Are you keeping your hands down as you turn, and as you make corrections with the lead?
- Are you using the same command-correction-command pattern as you did for the Heel exercise?

Heeling in a Circle

Practice the Heel and About-Turn by walking in a circle, as well as in a straight line. The circle has certain advantages: When you are on the outside of the circle, you are walking counter-clockwise and your dog has to slow down to adapt his stride to yours; when you are on the inside of the circle, you are walking clockwise and your dog has to move faster to stay alongside you. This change of pace is another way to coordinate his movements with yours.

9

Turning Corners, the Automatic Sit

Learning Time: One Week

BEFORE YOU BEGIN this lesson, spend a few minutes reviewing the Sit, Heel and About-Turn. From this point on, begin each lesson by reviewing all the previous exercises you and your dog have learned. This is how to achieve fluidity and, eventually, perfection.

TURNING CORNERS

When I train my students to turn left or right with their dogs, I insist that they make sharp, 90-degree turns. That is why these turns are called Corners. But someone always brings up the fact that when people are out walking with their dogs, they rarely have to make a 90-degree turn. Why, then, do I want them to turn in such a precise manner?

Practical Application

The 90-degree turn develops better coordination between you and your dog. It teaches the dog to concentrate on you and look for the movement that will tell her what you are going to do next. It also makes sense in your everyday life. Suppose, for instance, that you and your dog are walking down the street. Your dog is heeling at your left side. When you come to the corner, you decide not to cross the street and instead turn left to go around the block. If you and your dog haven't practiced making precise 90-degree turns, your dog will keep on walking in a straight line—she doesn't know how to read your body language and has no way of knowing that you are going to turn. The result: You will trip over her. It takes only a second for such an accident to happen. If your dog has been taught how to make 90-degree turns, she will have a quick response to your body language and will coordinate her motion with yours even when you make a slower, more rounded turn.

The Mechanics

Command your dog to heel and walk in a straight line. When you decide to turn right, repeat the Heel command. As your *left* foot hits the ground, pivot on it, turning your body precisely 90 degrees to the right, and step off to your right on your *right* foot, *without hesitation*. This is another exercise you should practice without your dog until you can do it smoothly.

Eventually, pivoting on your left foot will signal your dog that you are going to turn right and she will adjust her movement to yours. But in the beginning she won't know what to do. She will probably keep moving in a straight line, and you must snap your lead to correct her. At the same time, correct her verbally by saying, "No, Heel."

Your lead has to be in the proper position when you turn a corner. If you pull it across or up, you will pull your dog into your right leg, and that is incorrect. If your dog moves straight ahead when you turn right, keep your arms down and snap the lead with your left hand to bring your dog's attention back to you. Say "No, Heel" as you snap. You may have to snap the lead a few times to show your dog that you want her to be parallel to your left leg even when you turn in another direction. Give the verbal correction and command each time. As soon as she lines up with you and heels correctly in the new direction, praise her.

Walk ahead and execute another right turn. Continue this pattern until you complete a square and come back to where you began your Corners. Vary the size of the square to the size of the dog. For instance, with a Great Dane you might walk ahead about 30 feet before turning a corner; for a Chihuahua, 10 feet will be sufficient. If you make the square too big for your dog, you will tire her too quickly; if it is too small, she won't have enough space to turn properly.

Switch now to practicing the left turn. You are heeling in a straight line and decide to turn left. As you come down on your *right* foot, pivot on it, turning your body precisely 90 degrees to the left, and step out on your *left* foot, without hesitation.

You won't have a tendency to pull the lead across you when making a left turn, but you will tend to pull the lead back with your left hand to get it and your dog out of the way as you turn. This is a very common mistake, and you can work on correcting it without your dog.

If you see that your dog is in your way when you turn left, bump her with your left knee and give only the verbal correction "No, Heel." If your dog is small, brush her with your shoe (never the toe), just as you did when she was crowding you as she heeled. She will soon learn to stay out of your way and come into the heel position beside you as you move ahead. If she lags behind, snap the lead forward and say "No, Heel." Praise her when she turns the corner correctly. She will probably do it sooner than you do, because an animal's coordination is better than a person's. That is why we have to practice harder.

The Checklist

- Are you pivoting on the proper foot as you Corner? (Pivot on left to turn right; on right to turn left.)
- Are you raising the lead or pulling it across your body as you turn right? (As you pivot, your dog should stay with you but should not touch you. If you are raising or pulling the lead, you are causing your dog to walk into you. Keep the lead down.)
- On the left turn, are you using your knee or your shoe to correct your dog?

- When making corrections, are you saying "No" and following it with a Heel command?

THE AUTOMATIC SIT

Practical Application

When your dog is heeling by your left side and you stop for any reason, your dog should always stop instantly and sit by your side, her front legs parallel to your left knee. This is known as the Automatic Sit because your dog stops and sits when you stop, without being commanded to sit. If you are walking along a street and decide to look in a shop window, you should be able to stop and know that your dog will stop with you for as long as you stand there. She is comfortable in the Sit position. She is relaxed, yet ready to execute your next command. When you decide to move on, you can simply say your dog's name, give the Heel command, go on your way or go in another direction. When you come to a corner, you stop and your dog stops with you without being told. It is a very practical, handy exercise that enables you and your dog to work as a team.

The Mechanics

Your objective is to teach your dog how to read your body, know when you are going to stop moving, and sit alongside you the moment your forward motion ceases.

Begin with your dog heeling at your side. You should be holding the lead properly in your right hand, with your left hand approximately halfway down the lead (depending upon the size of the dog), taking up the slack.

When you decide where you are going to stop, you must move quickly and smoothly. Before you actually stop, slide your left hand up the lead toward your right hand, bring your right hand around, with your fingers open and your thumb through the loop, and take hold of the lead on the double-stitching. The back of your right hand should face outward and your thumb should be in the up position. Continue walking in that position for a few steps; you don't want your dog to take her cue to Sit from your hand movements, but rather when you give the Sit command.

100

Proper Sit position, small dog

Proper Sit position, large dog

As you stop on your *left* foot, your left hand should move toward the dog's croup (between the hip sockets), your fingers closed and pointing down toward the dog's tail. Simultaneously bring your right foot up to your left, bend your knees, and push down on the dog's croup with your left hand as you snap the lead up directly toward your nose with your right hand. Your right hand on the double stitching of the lead is controlling the front part of the dog's body and your left hand on the dog's croup is controlling the back. As you drop the dog into the Sit position, give the command to "Sit." You will have to bend your knees to do this properly; the smaller your dog, the deeper your bend. Don't use your dog's name when you give this command. Just say "Sit."

With the dog in the Sit position, her front legs should be parallel to your left leg. She should be sitting close to you but without touching you, and in a straight line with your body. To get moving again, you can give the Heel command or you can say "Okay" and end the lesson. Be sure to praise your dog when you finish.

This exercise will take some practice on your part, because if you aren't aligned with your dog when you issue the Sit command or if you don't handle the lead properly, she won't be in the proper Sit position described above. She can do this exercise correctly only if you do.

The Checklist

- Was your dog heeling properly before you stopped, her head parallel to your left leg?
- Did you stop on your left foot, bring up your right foot, bring your right hand over and grasp the lead in one smooth motion?
- Did you bend your knees as you reached down and placed your left hand on your dog's croup? Did you snap the lead up directly toward your nose with your right hand and give the Sit command?
- Did you practice this series of motions without your dog so you could do them smoothly when you worked with her?

10

Sit-Stay, Beginning the Hand Signals

Learning Time: One week

WHEN YOU GET to the point in your training when you are ready to learn the Sit-Stay, you will begin to use your hands as well as your voice to command your dog. Eventually, if you choose, you will be able to command your dog by using only your hands.

Some people are very impressed by hand signals because they think they are an advanced form of training. Actually they are really quite simple to master and you can begin to use them in the basic on-lead exercises.

WHAT HAND SIGNALS MEAN

Hand signals are not a replacement for verbal commands. Think of them as an alternative command for *some* situations, not all. For instance, you can't use hand signals at night because your dog won't be able to see them. And if you are a considerable distance away from your dog and he isn't looking at you, you will need a verbal command to get his attention.

There are two good reasons for using hand signals. First, they give you a chance to show off your dog—and there is nothing wrong with that, especially if the two of you have worked very hard to achieve your training goals. More important, however, hand signals teach your dog to concentrate on you. He learns that if he doesn't keep his eyes on you, you may give him a command, and when he doesn't execute it, he will be corrected.

Since the Sit-Stay is the first exercise that requires you to move away from your dog, this is the appropriate time to begin learning hand signals.

SIT-STAY

Practical Application

The Sit-Stay exercise allows you to control your dog from a distance; in fact, you will even be able to control him when you are out of his sight for a short period of time. In our modern world, there are very few occasions when you will want to leave your dog outside a store while you go inside for a moment, but if your dog is trained to Sit and Stay in place on command, you could do that. One of my students finds the Sit-Stay useful when she leaves her dog on command outside her house while she walks down to her mailbox, which is on a very busy road. The dog can see what she is doing, but he is away from the heavy traffic. More commonly, you can use the Sit-Stay when you are busy doing something around your house or yard and want your dog with you, but don't want him to wander around at will. It is a comfortable position for him to maintain for more than a few minutes, yet he is still under your control.

The Sit-Stay is also the first step in the Recall, a more complicated exercise that you will be learning later.

The Mechanics

Begin with your dog in a Sit position at your left side. You should be standing still. Hold the lead in your right hand, as usual.

You are now going to do a few things that are exactly the opposite of what you have been doing so far! Transfer the loop end of the lead to your *left* hand. Do not step out on your left foot. Pivot 180 degrees on your left foot, bringing your body around to face your dog. At the same time, bring your right foot around and across the front of your dog; bring your right hand around, fingers down, in front of your dog's face—but not touching him—and give the command "Stay." All these motions must be done quickly and smoothly or your dog will get up and try to move with you. The command must accompany, *not follow*, your foot movements and hand signal. You will have to practice these movements without your dog until you are comfortable doing them rapidly and simultaneously.

Don't leave your hand in front of the dog or he will probably reach out and sniff it. Drop it to your side.

With the lead still in your left hand, slowly back away from your dog until the lead is extended and only slightly bowed. The lead should not be pulled taut, or your dog will come toward you.

While in the Sit position, the dog should be sitting up straight, with his hindquarters square. He is allowed to move his head and his tail, nothing else. He is not allowed to sniff the ground.

Wait about ten seconds. Then begin to walk back to your dog, transferring the lead to your right hand again, with your thumb through the loop. Use your left hand to take up the slack as you approach the dog, with the palm of your hand toward the dog and the lead between your index finger and thumb. Do not pull the lead taut or your dog will think you want him to move.

You are *not* going to cross in front of the dog to get to his right side. Instead, you are going to pass by the dog on his left side, walk behind him and come back around to his right (your left) side. To do that, you must lift the lead with your left hand and hold it steady over the dog's right side at the same time you are passing along his left side. If your dog is large, you will have to lift the lead up high enough to avoid brushing the dog's head. Keep a slight bow in the lead portion between the dog's collar and your left hand. He should not feel that he is being held in place by the lead; eventually he should fccl that he is held in place by your command.

As you come back to stand beside your dog, drop your left hand from the lead and take up the slack with your right hand. Stand still, with your dog in the Sit position, and don't say anything. Wait a few seconds, then say "Okay!" enthusiastically, breaking the command. Or you can say "Okay!" and step forward quickly, ending the exercise by allowing your dog to go off command. Be sure to praise him.

The mechanics of this exercise aren't difficult for you, but they

Backing away from the dog

are for your dog. You are not only walking away from him, but you are walking behind him where you are out of his sight for a second or two. This is something very new for him, so don't expect him to stay in place right away. He may break repeatedly in the beginning, but if you correct him patiently, he will begin to realize that even though you are going away from him, you are coming back.

Don't expect to complete this exercise the first time you try it. You may not be able to back away from your dog for the first few days because he keeps breaking. Be patient. You may only be able to pivot and cross your right foot in front of him before he breaks. Give him plenty of encouragement any time he makes the slightest progress.

Naturally, as the dog masters the Sit-Stay, you won't have to keep on walking backwards when you leave your dog. It makes sense to do this in the beginning because you can see when your dog breaks and correct him immediately. But once you are doing the exercise smoothly, you can turn your back as you walk away from your dog and turn to face him when you reach the end of the lead.

When you are able to move away from him to the end of the lead, gradually increase the amount of time you stand still before walking back to him. Begin with two seconds and work your way up. He may break often at this point. But by the end of one week, he should be able to stay in place for about two minutes. By the end of the second week, he should hold for three minutes.

It takes at least two weeks for this exercise to become second nature for you and your dog. You both may be able to go through the mechanics smoothly after the first week, but you will need to practice longer if you want your dog to execute the command without even thinking about it—or in the presence of distractions.

HAND SIGNALS

At this point, you should begin using the hand signal for the Heel command as well as for the Sit-Stay. For at least the first week of the Sit-Stay lesson, use the hand signal along with the verbal command to give your dog a chance to associate one with the other.

Signaling the Heel:

Use your left hand to give this signal. Coordinate it with the action of stepping forward on your left foot as you give the verbal Heel command. At first this may feel awkward because it is natural for people to swing the right hand forward when the left foot steps out, so it may take a while before you can do it comfortably.

Your left hand should be at your side before you step forward. Do not swing it back and wind up. Just bring it forward from your side, palm forward, fingers closed, as your left foot steps out and you give the command "Heel."

Your dog will pick up hand signals in much the same way as he picks up verbal commands. If you give the commands in a sloppy manner, your dog will respond in a sloppy manner. If you give the hand signals sharply, your dog will respond sharply. Therefore, don't wave your left hand forward when you command your dog to heel. Bring it forward decisively.

Signaling the Sit-Stay

Follow the mechanics described above, and be precise in your motion. Swing your hand forward and drop it back to your side.

Corrections

If you are in front of your dog and he makes a mistake (such as breaking the Sit-Stay), always return to your dog and make the correction from his side. Don't pull him toward you or make a correction from in front of him. (This will carry over into the Recall, when you command your dog to come to you. He won't come to you willingly if he knows you are going to correct him when he gets there.)

If your dog begins to break as soon as you pivot and bring your hand across to signal him to stay, snap him back into the Sit position. If he continues to break, work only on your pivot and hand signal—along with your verbal command—until he holds the Sit position.

If your dog breaks when you walk away, walk back to him and snap him into the Sit position, say "No!" sternly and repeat the command to stay, using the hand signal with the verbal command. Walk away and stand at the end of the lead, no matter how many

Hand signal for Sit-Stay

times it takes for you to do it without your dog breaking the position.

If you are standing at the end of the lead and your dog lowers his head to the ground (not allowed), walk back to him and stand at his side. Bring his head up by snapping the lead upward, say "No" and repeat the command (verbal and hand signal) to stay. Walk away again.

As you walk back toward your dog, he will probably break the first several times. Remember, he is anxious because you walked away from him. Don't overlook or excuse the break. And don't correct him from in front. Get over to his side and correct him patiently, snapping him into the Sit position. Go out to the end of the lead and try again. Keep doing it until your dog holds the position long enough for you to get back to his side without correcting him.

When you return to his side, remain in the Heel position for a few seconds before releasing your dog from the command. This short pause will teach your dog not to break from the command until you release him verbally.

The Checklist

- As you began this exercise, did you take the lead in your *left* hand?
- As you gave the Stay command, did you:
  Pivot on your left foot?
  Bring your right foot across in front of your dog?
  Extend your right hand downward, fingers straight, palm facing your dog's head?
- Did you drop your right hand back to your side?
- Did you allow the lead to bow slightly when you stood at the end of it away from your dog?
- Did your dog sit straight up, with hips squared?
- Did he drop his head and sniff the ground?
- Did you correct him by walking back to him and standing by his side before you snapped the lead?
- When you walked back to your dog, did you take the lead in your right hand again? Did you use your left hand to hold the lead up over the dog's right side while you passed along his left side, behind him and around to his right side again?
- Did you wait a few seconds at your dog's side before ending the exercise?

11

Stand, Weave

Learning Time: One week

STAND

Practical Application

The Stand is a command you may not use often, but it has several advantages for everyday life. If you are out walking with your dog on a rainy day and you stop at a corner, your dog will get wet and muddy if he does the Automatic Sit beside you. Instead, you can command him to stand while you wait for the traffic to stop. You can do the same thing if you stop for any other reason.

Taking your dog to a veterinarian can be a chaotic experience if your dog sits down or tries to jump off the examining table every time the veterinarian touches him. When you can command him to stand while he is on the table, the examination will go much more quickly and pleasantly.

Since your dog will not be as comfortable standing as sitting— you wouldn't be either—don't put him on a Stand for a long period of time. Use the Sit-Stay command instead. Thirty seconds is very good; a full minute is exceptional at this stage of training. Eventually this time can be increased.

The Mechanics

Begin the Stand with your dog in the Sit position beside you. Hold the loop end of the lead in your right hand, as usual.

Pivot on your left foot and face the right side of your dog. Take the double-stitched part of the lead (at the clasp end) in your right hand, fingers closing around it (your thumb should still be through the loop). It is important to keep your right hand below the dog's head and not to pull on the lead. If you hold the lead up or pull it taut at this point, your dog will feel the tension and think you want him to sit.

Bring your right foot around in line with your left foot, but keep your feet apart. In a moment you will learn how to estimate how far apart your feet should be.

Drop your left hand down, palm up and fingers closed, and place it on your dog's stomach. Next, you are going to lift your dog's hind end up with your left hand and pull the lead *forward*, *not up* with your right hand. If you are working with a small dog, you will have to kneel or crouch down to do this properly. Normally I tell you not to pull the lead, but this is an exception to that rule. You are actually lifting and pulling the dog onto his feet and into the Stand. As you begin to do this, give the command "Stand." Be sure not to pull the lead up when you move him into a standing position. If you make that mistake, your right hand will be telling him to sit while your left hand tells him to stand. That will confuse your dog.

When your dog stands up, let him take at least one full step forward. That is a natural thing for him to do in order to achieve good balance. As he does this, lean a bit toward your right leg so you maintain control of him with the lead. After you do this a few times you will be able to gauge how far apart your own feet should be when you begin this exercise. The distance will depend upon the size of your dog.

As soon as your dog is in the Stand position, release the pressure on his collar by moving your right hand back toward him. This will let him know that he is doing the exercise correctly. Also check to see that your dog is in a comfortable standing position. If he isn't comfortable, you can't expect him to execute your command properly because he will be off balance. If he isn't standing properly, move him another step forward—you are controlling his hind end with your left hand and his front end with your right hand on the lead,

Standing the dog

so you should be able to move him easily. He should move with you and be in a better, more natural standing position.

Take your hand off your dog's stomach. Move it to your dog's right hind leg, palm toward the leg, and place your fingertips on his right knee. Apply a *little* pressure; it tells him not to move, which he will probably want to do. In the beginning it may be necessary for you to use the Stay command at this point until your dog learns to stay in the Stand. If you are going to walk away from your dog, always give him the Stay command and be sure to step out on your *right* foot, so that your dog knows he is not supposed to follow you.

Return to the Heel position beside your standing dog. Wait a few seconds, then call your dog's name, hesitate and give the command to Heel. Step forward on your left foot, bring your right foot up to your left foot and stop. This will bring your dog into a Sit by your side. The exercise is completed and your dog deserves your praise.

Hand Signal. Wait until you and your dog can do the Stand exercise smoothly before working the hand signal into it, because in the early part of your training you will need both hands to position your dog.

The hand signal is simple. With your dog in a Sit by your side, take the lead in your left hand and extend your right, palm up and fingers closed, toward your dog. Don't touch him, and keep your hand below his head. Then draw your hand back and away from your dog, lifting the fingers as if you were beckoning him in that direction. Do this at the same time that you give the command "Stand."

After that, the exercise is the same as in the Sit-Stay. With the lead in your left hand, use your hand signal and your voice to command your dog to Stay, step off on your right foot and walk backward away from your dog. Feed the lead out as you back up as far as the lead allows, letting it bow slightly. Stand facing your dog. Wait a few seconds and return to your dog exactly as you did in the Sit-Stay: Take the lead in your right hand, take up the slack with your left hand and use your left hand to lift the lead up and past the right side of your dog as you pass by him on his left side. Go around behind your dog, holding the lead steady at the dog's right side with your left hand, and come back to the Heel position beside your dog.

Wait a few seconds in place. Call your dog's name, give the verbal and hand signal commands to Heel, take one step forward on

Returning to Heel position

117

your left foot, bring your right foot up to your left foot and stop. Your dog should be in the Automatic Sit at your side. This ends the exercise, and you can now praise your dog.

Gradually increase the amount of time you stand opposite your dog while he is standing. Begin with a few seconds and increase to thirty seconds. The important part of this exercise is not how long your dog stands but how steady he is while he stands.

Much of this lesson repeats what your dog and you have learned while doing the Sit-Stay. The only difference is that your dog must learn to stand still rather than sit still. You should be doing it smoothly after a week. When that happens, ask a friend or a member of your family to come up to your dog and touch him while he is on command in the Stand and you are standing away in front of him. Ask the person to run his hands over the dog, similar to the way a judge would touch a dog in the Stand for Examination portion of a conformation or obedience show. A judge, however, usually touches only the dog's head, body and hind quarters. To prepare your dog for a visit to a veterinarian, ask your friend or family member to examine the dog more carefully, touching the dog's head, chest, back, stomach, the hind quarters, legs and feet, even his tail.

Corrections

If your dog breaks at any point in this exercise, go back to his side, make the correction, command him to sit and begin the entire exercise again.

The Checklist

- Did you pivot on your left foot and turn to face your dog's side?
- Was your right hand below your dog's head? Was your left hand on his stomach, palm up, fingers closed?
- Did you lift your dog into a Stand by pulling forward—not upward—on the lead with your right hand and lifting up his hind end with your left hand?
- Did you give the command to stand as you used your hands?
- Did you release the pressure on his collar with your right hand when he stood up?
- Did you return to Heel position before you walked away

from your dog? Did you wait a few seconds before giving the command (verbal and hand) to stay? Did you remember to feed the lead out as you backed away?

- When you returned to your dog, was the lead in your right hand, with your left hand taking up the slack? Did your left hand pass the lead along the dog's right side while you passed along his left side? Did you hold the lead steady with your left hand as you came around behind your dog and returned to Heel position at his right side?
- Did you wait a few seconds?
- Did you then call the dog's name, command him to heel, take one step forward and stop? Was your dog sitting by your side in an Automatic Sit? Did you praise him?

WEAVING

Practical Application

You and your dog know how to make left- and right-angle turns, but now you are going to learn how to weave around obstacles, such as people, lamp posts, telephone poles, opening doors, bicycles and all the other things that you might meet as you walk down a street together. Instead of turning sharply, you will turn in a more normal, curving manner.

The exercise is based on walking in a figure eight around and between two obstacles. This will continue to develop your coordination with each other.

The Mechanics

Begin with two portable objects, such as boxes or chairs, and place them about eight feet apart.

With your dog sitting beside you, give the Heel command and step forward on your left foot, as usual. Walk a figure eight, weaving in and out around the two obstacles, making sure that your dog's head is aligned with your left leg at all times. He will have to increase his pace when he is on the outside of a turn and decrease it when on the inside, but this is how his coordination improves.

Gradually move the two obstacles closer together until you

have only enough space for you and your dog to complete the figure eight without touching the obstacles. A Chihuahua will require less space than a Rottweiler, so the minimum distance will be determined by the size of your dog.

As you progress, speed up your pace until you are moving at a trot. Speed develops better coordination and encourages your dog to respond to your movements automatically, without thinking about what he is going to do. Stop periodically to reinforce the Automatic Sit.

To vary the exercise, weave in and out around at least two trees or objects, or ask two of your friends to stand opposite each other. Use as many objects or people as you wish. If your friends have dogs trained to sit, ask them to participate. Weaving in and out around other animals is a wonderful way to build up your confidence and teach your dog how to get along in your world.

Corrections

Use the same corrections you used for the Heel exercise. If your dog forges, lags or heels wide, be sure to snap the lead in the proper direction. If he crowds you, bump him with your knee or brush him with your foot.

The Checklist

- Did your dog maintain the proper Heel position as you did the figure eight?
- Did he touch the obstacles as you walked around them? Did you allow him enough space to clear them?
- When you stopped, did your dog go into the Automatic Sit?
- Was your dog distracted when you walked around people instead of obstacles? Was he distracted by other dogs?
- When he made a mistake, did you correct him properly and repeat the Heel command?
- Did you do the figure eight at a trot?

12

Down

Learning Time: One week

$\mathbf{T}$HE DOWN EXERCISE IS more difficult for your dog than it is for you, and at first it may be depressing to her. Although she may be comfortable lying around your house, she picks the time and place to lie down. Now you are going to give her a command that means, "Down—in this spot—don't move." Like any other animal, your dog is vulnerable in the Down position and she knows it. If she were attacked or surprised while she was lying down, it would take her longer to get up and defend herself. That primitive awareness is still part of her, so you can't expect her to drop down eagerly just because you tell her to do it. Once she adjusts to the command and learns that nothing is going to happen to her while she is down, she will gain confidence in herself and you will notice a change in attitude.

Practical Application

When you need to have your dog in one place, under your control, for a long period of time, you can give her the Down command. It will be more comfortable for her than the Sit-Stay or the

Stepping in front of the dog

Walking to the end of the lead

Stand. If you are visiting friends and you don't want your dog to wander around their house, use the Down command. You will have a more enjoyable visit.

The Mechanics

Your aim in this lesson is to give the Down command and have your dog drop to the Down position immediately, whether she is walking, running or standing still. To get to that level of achievement, you will have to proceed step by step. You are asking a lot of your dog, so be patient with her.

Depending upon your dog's temperament and size, you may encounter some problems teaching your dog this exercise. Consequently, I'm including several different techniques for you to try. Use the one that is most comfortable for both you and your dog. Working from your dog's side will give you more control (Techniques A and B), but if your dog is restless getting into the Down position, she may feel more secure with you in front of her (Technique C).

Technique A

This technique is especially recommended for large dogs.

Begin with your dog sitting by your side. Drop down on your left knee, facing the same way your dog is facing. Put your left hand on the double stitching of the lead, palm down and the back of your hand up. Lay your forearm across your dog's shoulder.

With your right hand, reach behind your dog's front legs and turn your palm outward toward the pasterns (what you might call her wrists). Take her left pastern in your right hand. Give the command "Down." As you do this, move your right hand forward (holding the dog's left pastern), bringing your forearm against the dog's right pastern, and move the dog's legs out from under her in a steady motion. (If you don't take the dog's left pastern in your right hand, the dog will simply step back over your arm as you move it forward.) Move your right leg forward the distance of one step. Put some weight on your left forearm (which is across your dog's shoulders) and push your dog into the Down position. When she gets into that position, stop pushing on her and place your left hand on her shoulder blades. Apply a little pressure, but not a lot, to keep her in place. If she can't get her front legs back under her shoulders, she won't try to get up.

Begin to stand, keeping your hands on your dog's shoulders while you feel her resisting. When you feel her relax, straighten up to the Heel position.

From this point on, the mechanics are the same as the Sit-Stay and the Stand-Stay: Pivot on your left foot, bring your right foot over and across the front of your dog, say "Stay" and use the Stay hand signal with your right hand. Back up, feeding out the lead, and stand facing your dog.

If your dog is in the proper Down position, her front legs are straight out in front of her and her hindquarters are tucked up underneath her body as they would be in a Sit. Some people find it acceptable if the dog's hindquarters roll over, but I prefer to see them square. The dog can get up more easily and quickly when the hindquarters are tucked under her.

When you are standing facing your dog, wait a few seconds before you return to her. Gradually build up this time to several minutes. Your dog may be restless at first, but the position itself is comfortable for her. When you return, follow the mechanics for the Sit-Stay and the Stand-Stay.

When you return to the Heel position beside your dog, wait a few seconds with your dog still in the Down. Vary this waiting time as you progress, so that your dog learns to wait for the command before standing up. Then call your dog's name, pause briefly, give the command "Heel," use the Heel hand signal, take one step forward with your *left* foot, bring your right foot up to your left and stop. Your dog should stand up and go into the Heel position alongside you. This is definitely the time to praise her.

Technique B

You won't get as much control using this technique because you will be bringing your dog down while in front of her, but some dogs are more comfortable doing it this way.

Begin with your dog sitting alongside you. Give her the command to stay and step out in front of her, facing her, still holding the lead in your right hand. Don't stand too close. Give yourself enough room to bring your dog into the Down position.

Kneel down on one knee; it doesn't matter which one. You will need both hands for this exercise, so let the loop end of the lead lie on the floor where you can retrieve it quickly if you need it.

Place your hands on the back of your dog's front legs, with your fingers below the elbow joints and your thumbs in front, in the elbow joints. As you give the command "Down," turn your wrists inward, pull your hands toward you, apply pressure on the front of your dog's legs with your thumbs and bring her into the Down position in front of you. Move backward if you don't have enough space.

Use the Stay command, stand up and back away from your dog to the end of the lead, as in the Sit-Stay and Stand-Stay. Complete the exercise in the same manner.

Technique C

This technique works well with smaller dogs.

Begin with your dog sitting at your side. Kneel down on your left knee, facing the same way your dog is facing. Lay the lead across your right thigh. You will need both hands free for this exercise.

Place your left hand on your dog's shoulders. Open the fingers of your right hand and bring your hand in *front* of your dog's front legs. Place your index finger between both front legs at the pasterns (wrists). Wrap your thumb around the dog's right front leg, so that your thumb and index finger are holding the dog's leg. Close your second finger (middle finger) around the dog's left front leg.

Give the command "Down," press down lightly on the dog's shoulders with your left hand, and pull the front legs out from under her with your right hand. Take your dog down quickly and firmly, but be careful not to slam her down, or you will reinforce rather than relieve her anxiety about the Down exercise.

Complete the exercise as for Sit-Stay and Stand-Stay.

Corrections

Again, *never* correct your dog from in front. This is especially important to remember as you get into more difficult exercises. While it may tax your patience to go back to your dog, correct her and repeat the exercise from the beginning, be sure to do it every single time she makes a mistake or breaks from the command. This is the only way to communicate your disapproval without weakening the trust that has been built between the two of you.

Remember, too, to end your training periods with an exercise your dog can perform well. Praise her at every opportunity, because that will carry her through the difficult times and make her eager to do her best.

The Checklist

Technique A

- Did you turn to your left and face your dog? Did you leave some space between your left and right foot so you wouldn't be off balance when you pulled your dog down?
- Did you kneel down, bend your left arm back toward you, and put your left forearm across your dog's shoulders and your right hand, palm forward, behind her pasterns?
- Did you press down with your left arm and move your dog's front legs out as you gave the command "Down"?

Technique B

- Did you command your dog to stay before you moved in front of her?
- Did you leave enough space in front of you to bring her legs down?
- Did you hold your dog's front legs properly, fingers below the elbows, thumbs in the elbow joint? Did you turn your wrists inward and move the dog's legs forward and down as you gave the command "Down"?

Technique C

- Did you kneel down on your left knee beside your dog?
- Did you place your left hand on your dog's shoulders?
- Did you hold your dog's front legs with the thumb and fingers of your right hand, thumb and index finger around the right front leg, second finger around the left front leg?
- Did you give the command "Down" as you pulled forward and brought the dog's front legs out from under her?

All Techniques

- Did you complete the exercises in the same way as for Sit-Stay and Stand-Stay?
- Did you make all corrections from beside your dog?
- Did you praise her at the end of the exercise?

Developing a Fluid Motion

When you see that your dog knows how to achieve the Down, you can stop kneeling beside her and using your hands. Begin the exercise with your dog in a Sit by your left side and give the command "Down." If she doesn't respond immediately, make the correction with a "No!" snapping the lead at the same time, and kneel down on your left knee. Take her down quickly. Return to the Heel position. From this point on, proceed as in the Sit-Stay and Stand-Stay exercises. It will take a while before your dog will drop down on the command, but don't settle for anything less. Always do the complete exercise after making a correction so that your dog learns to perform it in its entirety.

Down from the Heel Position

When your dog is responding well to the Down command from a Sit, begin doing the exercise while the dog heels. Your goal should be to teach your dog to drop instantly on command. To make your point, you will have to move very quickly and decisively.

Command your dog to heel and work up to a fast Heel. When you are ready, give the command "Down," put your left hand on the double-stitched part of the lead, stop and go down on your left knee in one fluid motion, snapping the lead downward with your left hand and talking your dog into a Down alongside you.

The first few times you do this exercise, you may have to command your dog to stay while you stand up. Heeling fast excites the dog and she will not want to stay still. Correct her if she breaks, put her back into the Down and tell her to stay while you stand up. Return to the Heel position and keep your dog down for a second or two. Correct her if she breaks and tries to sit. Then give the command to heel, take one step forward and stop, bringing your dog to a Sit by your side. The exercise is completed. Praise your dog.

To vary the exercise, command your dog to come, and as she does, step off to your right or left, bringing her into a Heel alongside you without coming to a stop.

Hand signal. Begin using the hand signal along with the verbal command after you and your dog are doing this exercise smoothly and your hands are relatively free. The signal is simple: Extend your right hand toward your dog, with your index finger pointing toward the ground.

Down from in Front

When you are facing your dog at half the distance of the lead, she will realize that you cannot control her with your hands. Consequently, the first few times you give the Down command, she may ignore it. To bring your dog into a Down while you are standing in front of her at the end of the lead—and eventually when you are even farther away—you must show her that you can indeed control her from where you are.

Begin with your dog sitting beside you. Give the command "Stay" and walk away from her, stepping out on your *right* foot and holding the loop end of the lead in your *left* hand (the reason for this will become apparent in a moment). When you reach the end of the lead, turn and face your dog. The lead should be almost, but not quite, taut. Pause briefly.

As you give the command "Down," do three things at the same time: Pull the lead taut with your left hand; pivot slightly to your left on your left foot; then raise your right leg (without bending the knee) higher than the lead, bring it across, turn your right foot toward the lead and step down hard on it, taking it down to the ground. Be sure to step slightly in toward your dog when you use this technique. If you step straight down, you will pull your dog toward you instead of teaching her to drop in place without moving forward. As your foot comes down on the lead, it must be aimed slightly toward your dog. In effect, this is a way of snapping the lead from a distance; it will bring your dog into the Down position. Her hindquarters may not be square and she may roll over a little, but she will realize that you can control her from a distance. Do this exercise as quickly as you can so that your dog doesn't have time to stand up after you give the command "Down." If she stands, go back to her side, make the correction and begin the exercise over again from the Heel. Praise her when she does it correctly.

Hand signal. After your dog goes into the Down position on command, without your foot on the lead, you can begin to use the hand signal. The Down hand signal from in front of your dog is different from the signal you used when standing beside her. Facing your dog, give the command "Down" as you bring your right arm up above your head, fingers closed, palm toward your dog.

The Checklist

- When you faced your dog, did you pause before giving the command?
- Was the lead in your *left* hand so that you could step on it effectively with your right foot to correct your dog? Was the lead almost taut? If you wear a shoe with a heel, you will have more control.
- To make the correction, did you raise your *right* leg and turn your *right* foot toward the lead as you brought it across and stepped down on the lead? Did you say "No" and repeat the command "Down" as you brought her down?

13

Recall

Learning Time: Two weeks

Practical Application

When you do the Recall, you call your dog to you, he comes immediately, at least at a trot, drops into a perfect Sit in front of you and, when given the command, moves into a Heel position by your side. Learning how to do the Recall is more complicated than the reason for doing it. This is why I advise allowing two weeks for this exercise.

Put very simply, the reason for the Recall is to get your dog to come to you when you call him. It is probably the most useful command you will ever learn. If you take your dog to a park for a little off-lead fun, you will want to be assured that you can call him to you when you are ready to go home. If he won't come to you, you can't leave. Even if you are out in your own backyard with your dog, you will want to be able to call him to you and know that he will obey your command. If you want to play ball with him, you will have to teach him to bring the ball back to you after you throw it, and that means he has to come to you. If you want to feed him and he is in another part of the house with the children, you won't have to go looking for him; you can call him to you.

Some dog owners make the mistake of thinking that all they have to do is call their dog and the dog will come to them. That won't happen, unless by accident, because very often the dog is interested in something else, such as a scent or another person or an animal on the horizon, and he hasn't been taught to ignore such things when a command is given. Consequently, the irate owner runs toward the dog, the dog looks up, sees the owner charging down on him and thinks, "Game time!" The dog then turns the chase into a game of tag, or comes running toward the owner and swerves away at the very last minute. This is not the way to control your dog. It is also not the way to protect him when you want to call him back from potential danger.

When your dog responds to your command by coming to you, he has to ignore distractions, and a dog won't do that naturally. He has to be trained to do it, and the training must be done in a step-by-step manner.

Many people skip the simpler basic exercises and try to go directly to the Recall. Then they wonder why their dog can't understand what they want him to do. The Recall isn't easy for the person or the dog, but it can be learned much more successfully if it follows the Heel, Sit, About-Turn, Automatic Sit, Sit-Stay, Stand and Down. Some of these exercises form the basis of the Recall.

Two important reminders: 1. Always call your dog's name before you give the command to come; and 2. Never, under any circumstances, call your dog to you to correct him. Always go to him and make the correction from his side.

The Recall is the most complicated and difficult of the basic exercises. For these reasons, I prefer to divide the mechanics into two parts: teaching your dog to come to you, and bringing him to the Heel position at your side.

The Mechanics—Part I

You and your dog have already learned the Sit-Stay. Begin the Recall by going through the Sit-Stay procedure. With the dog sitting at your left side, give the verbal command "Stay," and use the hand signal along with it, if you wish. Go out to the end of your lead, turn and face your dog. Transfer the lead to your left hand, because you will need to use your right hand for the hand signal. The lead should not be taut; let it go slightly slack.

Call your dog's name—you are going to give him a command to move, and you should always call his name before you do that. Hesitate. As you give the command "Come," snap the lead toward you and start running backward. *Run—don't walk.* How far and how fast you will have to run will depend upon the size and speed of your dog. A large dog will usually cover ground faster than a small dog, but a Fox Terrier may outrun a Bull Mastiff. The reason for running backward is to make your dog come to you at least at a trot, a requirement of the Recall. If your dog responds sluggishly, snap-and-release, snap-and-release the lead again and again as you continue to run backward. If you are moving faster than your dog, the lead will be taut; remember to move it in the direction of your dog to achieve a little slack, and then snap it back toward you and release it immediately. It will take a great deal of practice before you can coordinate *your* mechanics; then you will have to pay attention to your dog's. Work on yours without him, and you will find it much easier to teach him what he has to do.

If your dog comes toward you at a trot, he will cover ground faster than you do, so you will begin to get some slack in the lead. As this happens, and as your dog comes closer to you, grab the lead halfway down its length with your right hand. Continue backing up. Bring your left hand around (thumb still through the loop) and underneath the lead to grab it at the stitching enclosing the snap. Keep backing up, still running, until your dog is within twelve inches of your feet, perfectly straight in line with you. Stop. Let go of the lead with your right hand and bring your hand up to cup your dog's chin and the lead in your fingers, placing your right thumb across his nose. Your body will be bent slightly forward from the waist up. This technique is called "trapping the lead," because in one hand you are holding the lead and the dog's chin and muzzle. It gives you control of the dog's head and you can bring him into line with you.

As you stop, straighten up. Give the command "Sit" as you bring both elbows out, snapping the lead upward. This will bring both of your hands up in front of you. Once the dog sits properly, release his muzzle. Transfer the loop end of the lead back to your right hand. Your dog should be sitting directly and squarely in front of you, within twelve inches of your shoe tips. Eventually you can eliminate the Sit command in this part of the Recall, but in the beginning it's a good idea to use it because it will help your dog to understand what he is expected to do.

Since the Recall is the most complicated of the basic obedience commands, the following summary of the mechanics should make them easier to remember:

As you give the Come command, simultaneously snap the lead with your left hand and begin running backward as fast as you can. As your dog begins to come toward you, reach down with your right hand and take the lead halfway between your left hand and the double stitching, pulling it toward you and taking up the slack. Bring your left hand around and take the double stitching. Lay the lead snap and choker chain under the dog's chin; bring the right hand up, place four fingers under his chin and your thumb across the top of his muzzle. Snap the lead up, bringing the dog into a sitting position directly in front of you.

If your dog begins to drift to one side or the other as you are running backward, a correction must be made while you are still in motion. Snap the lead to you and in the direction opposite to your dog's drift. For example, if your dog is drifting toward your right as he comes toward you, snap the lead a little toward your left to bring him back in line. The best way to avoid drifting is to run backward fast enough so that your dog doesn't have the opportunity to drift.

A very common mistake is to praise the dog at this point. Please don't do it. Wait until the exercise is finished. Praise at this point will only distract your dog.

The Recall is a difficult exercise, because it requires a level of coordination you probably never had to master. Don't be discouraged if you start out clumsily. It will take a lot of practice before the motions feel natural. Keep in mind that your goal is to give your dog a signal that will make him come to you—*at least at a trot*—and sit directly in front of you. This is why, from the very beginning of the exercise, you must run backward quickly, or your dog will amble along toward you, getting there whenever he is good and ready.

Practice running backward without your dog until you can do it comfortably and without falling down. You may feel foolish if anyone sees you doing it all by yourself, but consider how great you will feel when you can call your dog to you and know he will come without hesitation.

Recall from Heel

You won't always be calling your dog to you from the Sit position. Sometimes you may want to call her when she's ahead of

you, behind you or off to one side. She may not be looking at you and your command may take her by surprise. To train her for these situations, you need to learn the Recall to Heel. Do this *after* the two of you have mastered the basic Recall.

Heel your dog. With the lead in your right hand, suddenly stop walking forward. Snap the lead as you begin running backward and give the Come command. Quickly transfer the lead to your left hand and snap the lead. From this point on, the mechanics are the same as the Recall exercise. If your dog doesn't turn around and begin coming toward you at least at a trot, repeat the snap-release as you continue running backward until she comes to you in a straight line.

When you begin to practice this exercise, complete it as in the basic Recall. Eventually, as you and your dog become more confident, vary the final mechanics by heeling to your right or left as your dog comes toward you, and either stop or continue walking with your dog at your side. And remember: Don't praise—yet.

This exercise will speed up your dog's response to your command and encourage her to focus her attention on you.

The Mechanics—Part II

Now you must bring your dog from directly in front of you to your left side and into Heel position. There are two ways to do it, to the left and to the right. The left is used more often.

Left Heel

Your dog is sitting directly in front of you, and you are holding the lead in your right hand.

Bring your left hand around and over the lead, bring the palm of your hand down over the lead, close your fingers on the lead (bringing the lead between your four fingers and the palm of your hand). Hesitate. Call your dog's name. Hesitate again. As you give the Heel command, step back on your left foot, snapping your left arm—elbow stiff—in a half-moon arc to your left. Bring your dog back far enough behind your left leg so that the dog can turn toward you and start coming up alongside you in a straight line. When your dog's head parallels your left leg, step forward on your left foot, transferring the lead to your right hand—your right hand taking the double stitching, and the back of your hand forward. As your right foot comes forward, even with your left, and your forward motion stops, sit the dog in the Automatic Sit. If you have a large dog you will have to exaggerate your backward step to bring her back far enough to turn and come up level with your leg. You will also have to lean back as you swing your arm in the arc. Keep your left arm stiff as you move it from the side and back, and as you bring it from in back to your side in a straight line. This will bring your dog in straight, too.

Avoid the tendency to pull your dog toward you as you run backward. Snap the lead and let it go slack as many times as necessary, but don't pull, or your dog will instinctively pull back away from you.

Right Heel

Use this method if you prefer to move your dog to the Heel position by moving her past the right side of your body and around to your left side.

With your dog sitting squarely in front of you, hold the lead in your right hand, above the double stitching (higher if your dog is small). Call your dog's name, hesitate, and give the command "Heel." As you do this, snap the lead with your right hand and simultaneously take one or two steps backward, depending upon the size of the dog. If you are taking one step back, step back on your right foot. If your dog is very large and you are taking two steps back, begin on the right foot and take two steps back. At the same time, transfer the lead behind your back from the right hand to the left hand as your dog comes around the right side of your body and crosses behind you. As your dog comes around to your left side, transfer the lead to your right hand, taking the double stitching. As your dog's head comes around your left knee, take a full step forward with your right foot. As you bring your left foot up to your right, reach back to the dog's croup with your left hand. From that point on, continue as in the Automatic Sit.

Heeling left or right is a matter of preference. Heeling left gives you a little more control over your dog because she doesn't have to go around you and you will have constant visual contact with her. If you heel right, you may be a bit off balance when stepping back on your left foot, and you can't see your dog when she is behind you, but the technique allows more maneuvering space when working with a very large dog such as a Newfoundland.

Heel Variations

When your dog is sitting in front of you, you may not want to wait for her to come around in an arc and sit beside you. You may want to go somewhere with your dog beside you, but without going into the sitting position. You can do that easily.

To heel right: With your dog sitting in front of you, give the command "Heel" as you step off to the right on your right foot. Use your Heel hand signal at the same time. Your dog will come right along beside you.

To heel left: With your dog sitting in front of you, give the command "Heel" as you turn and step off to the left on your left foot. Use your Heel hand signal. As you step off, quickly transfer the lead to your left hand behind your back and back again to your right hand once you are moving toward your left and your dog is coming up alongside you.

Corrections

Dogs are like people: They take shortcuts. For example, when you begin practicing the Recall, your dog will often come in and, instead of sitting in front of you, will whip around to your left side. Having done the exercise a few times, he knows he is going to end up at your left side, so he figures, *Why should I sit in front when I'm going to move around to the side anyway?*

You may even agree with the dog's point of view. But there is a reason why he should stop directly in front of you. It teaches him discipline. Sure, a shortcut makes sense to him, but you gave the command to do something else; your command is what must be obeyed, regardless of what his logical mind tells him to do.

If your dog comes in at an angle, heading for your side instead of directly in front of you, say "No" as you snap the lead and run backward again, repeating the command "Come." Repeat the exercise as many times as necessary until your dog does it correctly. Don't allow your dog to pass by you when he is coming in, because once he realizes he can get past you, he will do it again. Even if you have to run and stand in front of him to stop him, do it. Correct him and run backward, call his name and repeat the command "Come."

Be careful not to pull on the lead as you call your dog to you. If you pull, he will instinctively pull the other way. Snap the lead quickly and precisely to make him come to you on his own. If this is what you will want him to do when he is off lead, train him properly when he is on lead.

The Checklist

- Before you gave the command to come, did you call your dog's name and hesitate?
- Did you snap the lead and start running backward?
- As your dog came closer, did you grab the lead halfway down with your right hand, bring your left hand around and grab the lead below your right hand (the exact place will depend upon the size of the dog), and trap the lead under the dog's chin with your right hand, your thumb on the top of the dog's muzzle?
- Did you stop, release your dog's muzzle, bring your elbows out and your hands up in front of you, all at the same time?
- Did you transfer the lead to your right hand?
- Did you hold the double stitching on the lead with your left hand, keep your elbows straight and swing your left arm out in an arc as you gave the command to heel and stepped backward on your left foot?
- Did you bring your right foot back up alongside your left foot, bringing your dog to your side into a Sit?
- Did you take one step forward on your left foot, bring your right foot up to your left foot and stop?
- Did you give your dog a lot of well-deserved praise?
- If you brought your dog around to your right, did you take enough steps back to keep yourself in balance as your dog walked around you? If you took two steps, did you remember to step back on your left foot first so you would end on your right foot?
- Did you transfer the lead from your right hand to your left as your dog passed behind you, then back to your right when your dog came around to your left side?
- If your dog tried to pass by your left side to go to Heel position without stopping in front of you, did you run backward and bring her into a straight line by snapping the lead?
- If the dog heeled to the right, did you step out on your right foot as you gave the command to heel?
- If the dog heeled to the left, did you step out on your left foot as you gave the command to heel?

14

Evaluating Yourself and Your Dog

$\mathbf{B}$Y NOW you have gone through the basic Subnovice, or on-lead, exercises, and if you are like most of my students, you are eager to work off lead with your dog. Don't be in too much of a hurry. Be sure you are ready to move on, because if there are any weaknesses in your on-lead work, they will show up when you take your dog off lead.

As a preliminary to going on to Novice, or off lead, training, take your dog through all the exercises you have learned. Do it in one lesson, and set your standards high. This is not the same as competing in a show, where everyone's performance rates a score. In this test, you pass or fail.

The key to evaluating what you and your dog have accomplished so far is to be absolutely honest with yourself. If you and your dog can go through all the basic exercises on lead without needing a correction, you are ready to begin training your dog to work off lead. If, however, you have to correct your dog as you go through the basic on-lead exercises, don't make excuses for the mistakes. And don't blame your dog. If he is doing something wrong, the fault is yours. If, for instance, your dog isn't sitting properly, don't tell yourself he just isn't in the mood because it's a rainy day. Ask yourself *why* your dog isn't sitting properly. Then go back over the basic Sit exercise objectively, not judgmentally, until you find out what you did wrong. It can be something as simple as the way you handled the lead or the tone of your voice when you gave the command.

If you have always practiced with your dog in your own backyard or in the same neighborhood area, and if you have not exposed your dog to unfamiliar situations and challenges, then you are not ready to go on to off lead exercises no matter how well you and your dog perform. Both of you should be tested on lead many times before you attempt working off lead.

Don't let your mistakes discourage you. Let your imperfections bring you to perfection by pointing out what your weaknesses are. These are the areas where you need more practice. As a matter of fact, I always urge my students to *look* for their mistakes, because mistakes are our best teachers.

Going back over the on-lead exercises will also point out your accomplishments, and they will be many. Don't dwell on your mistakes; you can correct them. Pay attention to your successes and take pride in what you and your dog can do. Think back to where you were when you began your training, and you will be amazed at how far you have come. Remember when you used to call your dog and he went on sniffing the grass or walked the other way? Remember when you couldn't get him to sit, except when *he* wanted to? Or how about trying to take him for a walk and getting tangled in the lead? All the hours of practice, sweat and frustration will begin to fade from your memory once you are able to appreciate what you have accomplished.

To me, the greatest satisfaction that comes from working with a dog is the awareness that you can communicate with each other on a deeper, more satisfying level than you ever thought possible. When you truly become a team and begin to function as one instead of two, you will both know it. It is one of the finest relationships in the world.

PART III

TRUSTING EACH OTHER

Introduction
Step-by-Step
Novice Lessons
(Off Lead)

WHEN YOU BEGIN to work with your dog off lead, do it in a safe, confined area so that if your dog breaks and runs, she won't get hurt. Once you are comfortable working without a lead, take her into new and unfamiliar territories, just as you did when you were working with a lead. Expose your dog gradually to distractions and problems, and if she doesn't execute a command properly and immediately, don't hesitate to go back to your six-foot lead to improve her performance.

In most communities there are leash laws, and you should find out what they are, not only in your own neighborhood but wherever you plan to take your dog. They will vary from state to state. In some states, dogs must be on a lead unless they are under the owner's control, which is another way of saying that your dog can walk off lead if she is properly trained. But in many states your dog must be on a lead whenever she is away from your property. This restriction may make it difficult for you to find an area away from home where you can legally walk your trained dog off lead. But with a little planning and investigation, you can find a way to do it. A good way to begin is to call the local police department, parks department or conservation officer and ask where you can walk your dog off lead. You can also join a dog club to gain access to special areas available to members.

When you begin Novice, or off-lead, exercises, you don't simply take the lead off your dog. You have to do it in stages, not only for your dog's sake but for yours. You need to gain confidence in your ability to control your dog without a lead, and your dog has to realize that you still have authority over her. This takes time and a gradual approach to off-lead work. In my classes I break down this interval into: Letting Go of the Lead, the Grab Lead, the Intermediate Lead and the Crepe Paper Test. Finally, I tell my students to take the collar off the dog.

When you can command your dog to do all the basic exercises without a lead or even a collar, and without making a correction, you will have a trained dog—and your dog will have a trained owner.

15

Letting Go of the Lead

WHEN YOU FIRST BEGIN to work with your dog off lead you will probably be surprised to find that you have more control over your dog than you thought you had. Your dog will know immediately that the lead isn't there and he will behave differently. By that I don't mean he will run off and disappear. He now has enough training to know how to respond to your commands, so it is not as if you have an uneducated animal at your side. But he knows that you don't have the same kind of control over him, and he will test you. How he does that will depend upon the individual dog, his breed and you.

Now is the time for both of you to discover that your authority doesn't depend on being connected to your dog by a leather lead. Your authority really grows out of the relationship you have been building up through so many repetitious hours of training and learning from each other. You give the commands and your dog executes them, lead or no lead.

Of course, it will take a while before this transition goes smoothly. You will let go of the lead in stages, and you will always go back to it to solve problems. Each stage of letting go has two purposes: to reveal your weak points, so you can do more work where it's needed; and to build up your confidence by showing you how far you have come.

In this chapter you will gradually let go of your end of the lead by wrapping it around your waist and by draping it across your shoulder instead of holding the loop in your hand. The object of these exercises is to make you feel comfortable with your hands off the lead.

LEAD AROUND YOUR WAIST

Pass the loop end of the lead around your waist, run the clasp end through the loop, and fasten the clasp to your dog's collar.

Your dog will realize immediately that your hands aren't on the lead. But he's not stupid: He knows that *he* is still on the lead. This exercise is more for your benefit than your dog's. Once your hands come off the lead, you will be uncomfortable. You won't know what to do with your hands. When you give your dog a command, you will wonder, "Will he really do it?" At the same time, you will know that you can just reach out and snap the lead to control your dog. But the feeling is not the same as having the lead in your hand. That is why this exercise is important: It will show you that you can control your dog without holding onto him. You can walk along with your hands at your side in a perfectly normal position.

With the lead around your waist, take your dog through the Sit, Heel, About-Turn, Left and Right Corners and Weaving. With the lead around your waist, you won't have enough space to do the other exercises, but you will use different transitional methods with them.

Follow the step-by-step instructions in the Subnovice exercises, and go through the checklist at the end of each one. Don't hurry. Take the exercises one at a time. For instance, when you see that you and your dog are heeling well with the lead wrapped around your waist, go on to the About-Turn. If you make mistakes, correct them by snapping the lead and repeating the command, and even going back to your basic on-lead work if necessary. Then put the lead back around your waist and go on to the next exercise.

LEAD OVER YOUR SHOULDER

This exercise may not be possible if the dog is very small and the owner very tall because the lead will not reach the owner's

shoulder. If this is the case, the lead around the waist exercise will do very well.

With your dog in a Sit beside you with the lead fastened to his collar, drape the lead across your body and over your right shoulder, letting it rest there. You may be a bit apprehensive because you know that if your dog pulls away from you, you will have to move quickly to grab the lead. If such a thing should happen, you will feel a tug, and you will have enough time to catch the lead and control your dog—unless you are not paying attention. But remember that your dog already has had a lot of training and is not likely to go dashing off. This exercise is another confidence builder for you.

Go through the Sit, Heel, About-Turn, Left and Right Corners and Weaving with the lead over your shoulder. If you have to make several corrections, go back to the six-foot lead and the basics. Then return to the lead over your shoulder. When you can take your dog through the above exercises without making mistakes, you are ready to move on.

Here is something I will repeat many times: *When your dog doesn't obey a command off lead, put the lead on and go back to your basic exercises until you both perform them flawlessly. Then take the lead off again.* This is not an indication of your failure or your dog's. As long as you have your dog and as far as you go in training, there will be times when it makes sense to review the basics and sharpen your performance. The better you perform with the lead, the better you will perform without it.

16

The Grab Lead

THE GRAB LEAD is the loop end of a lead plus the clasp that fastens onto your dog's collar. It is nothing more than a handle. To gain control of your dog, you don't always have to put your hand through the loop; it is enough just to grab it.

The grab leads available in pet supply stores are made of leather, webbed cotton or nylon, and they are too large for small dogs. If you have a small dog, you can make your own grab lead: Cut a length of ordinary clothesline, tie the ends together to form a loop; slip the loop end through the ring in your dog's collar and pull the tied ends through the loop end. The tied ends should hang down on your dog's shoulder, forming a handle of sorts that you can easily grab. For some of the Toy breeds, such as a Miniature Pinscher, use nylon clothesline.

Use the grab lead only after you are comfortable with your hands off the standard lead. Technically, you are off lead; psychologically, you are not. As far as the dog is concerned, the grab lead reminds him of the lead because it constantly touches his shoulder as he moves. It reinforces his previous training and shows him that you still have control over him. It boosts your confidence, because even though you are not holding anything in your hand, you know you still have something you can reach down and hold onto in case your dog begins to break away from you.

If you have any leftover problems from your on-lead work, they will show up again now. For instance, if your dog tended to lag when heeling, he may lag even more when you begin using the grab lead, because he senses that your physical control over him is changing. Since you are working so much closer with him, however, you can correct him more forcefully. Now you are at the point where he has to learn. He has to realize that before you go to the next step, it simply isn't worth his effort to disobey your command. By this time your dog has learned the exercises and knows what to do, so he may be testing you by disobeying. You have to make it clear to him that it isn't worth the effort to do that, and it's much easier to do things your way.

Use the grab lead to go through the Sit, Heel, Fast Heel, About-Turn, Corners, Stand, Down and Weaving exercises. It isn't suitable for exercises that require you to move away from your dog. Begin in a sheltered area and gradually work up to areas that offer distractions. When your dog does not make any mistakes, you are ready to take the grab lead off.

The Mechanics

You will have to work close to your dog, so when you begin doing an exercise, hold the grab lead in your *left* hand instead of your right. As your dog responds to your commands, let go of the grab lead and let your hands drop to your sides in a normal manner as you continue the exercise.

The grab lead will drop and touch the dog's shoulder or chest. Your dog will know he is free, but he will be reminded that something is still attached to his collar.

Be careful not to get in the habit of reaching for the grab lead every time your dog moves. Use your voice first. Give your dog the command and correct him verbally if he doesn't perform properly. In most instances, you will still have time to reach the grab lead if your dog doesn't obey. If you need to make a correction with the grab lead, use either hand to grab the lead. Follow the usual procedure of saying "No," snapping the lead and repeating the command.

For Small Dogs

Be prepared to bend quickly and grab the lead if you need to make a correction. Don't worry about inserting your hand into the loop. Just reach for the knotted end—it is faster that way.

17

The Intermediate Lead

THE INTERMEDIATE LEAD can be twenty-five or fifty feet long. Twenty-five feet is more common. This lead allows you to evaluate your control over your dog from a distance and prepares you to let go of the lead entirely.

When you come to the Sit-Stay command, you will be walking farther away from your dog than you could while you were holding a six-foot lead. Eventually you will be training your dog to sit in one place and stay there while you walk out of his sight. Naturally, your dog will become uneasy when you begin to walk farther away, but with practice she will learn that you will come back. When you go out of her sight, however, she will probably try to follow you, because she wants to go with you. It takes time and patience to teach her that even when she can't see you, you still have control of her and you will return.

By using a twenty-five-foot intermediate lead, you can begin to walk some distance away from your dog, yet you will still be able to correct her if she breaks and tries to follow you. Sometimes, when you first go to the twenty-five-foot lead, it is advisable to put the grab lead on your dog as well. It reinforces your control over the dog as you begin to work farther away from her. When your dog holds the Sit-Stay command while you walk twenty-five feet away from her, you will be ready to go off lead entirely for this exercise. The intermediate lead can also be used for the Stand-Stay, Down-Stay and Recall.

The Mechanics

A common mistake is to begin with the dog in a Sit position and stretch the lead out directly in front of her. It may seem like a logical thing to do, but actually it isn't. If the lead is directly in front of the dog, it holds her in check because she will step on it and think you are making a correction when she feels the tug. Instead, bring the lead out to the dog's right side before stretching it out in front of her. You will appreciate this detail when you come to the Recall.

With your dog in the Sit position, you can begin the Sit-Stay in one of two ways: Fasten the lead onto your dog's collar and stretch it out away from her, or stretch the lead out and then fasten it onto her collar.

Give the command to stay and walk away from your dog by stepping off on the right foot, as you did in the Sit-Stay exercise, not by stepping off on your left foot, as you did in the Heel exercise. Don't back up; just walk away to the other end of the lead. Turn and face your dog.

If you are working with a large dog, don't stretch the lead out in front of her. Hold it in your hands and reel it out as you walk away. Then, if your dog breaks, you can check her more quickly because you will have some of the lead in your hands. Don't try to check her by stepping on the lead, or you may lose your balance.

If you are working with a small dog, stretch the lead out in front of her. If she breaks while you are walking away, step on the lead to stop her, and then go to her to make the correction.

When you reach the end of the lead, turn around and face your dog. Step on the lead in case your dog breaks and you need to check her.

Pause a few seconds, then return to your dog, go around behind her and come up on her right side. Pause. Complete the exercise by taking one step forward on your left foot as you give the command "Heel" and bring your right foot up to your left foot.

Go through the other Stay commands in the same way.

Going Out of Sight

The intermediate lead will enable you to put your dog in one of the Stay commands while you go out of her sight. There are two ways to do it.

1. Put your dog on a Sit-Stay command and go around the corner of a building, such as a garage or a shed, where you can look through a window and observe your dog's behavior. In this way you can correct your dog if she breaks the command.

Depending on the weather and the dog's temperament, it is sometimes helpful to start out with your dog in the Down position when you go out of her sight. She will be less inclined to break than in the Sit position.

2. Get the help of a friend who can sit in a car or stand at a distance and observe your dog's behavior when you go out of sight. Your friend should be in your sight so he or she can signal you if your dog breaks the command.

In the beginning, your dog may not stay for more than a few seconds after you go out of sight. If she tries to follow you or go off in another direction, correct her immediately and begin the exercise again. Expect to spend a lot of time repeating it before your dog will stay in place for as long as one minute.

At the end of the exercise, return to your dog exactly as you usually do in the Sit-Stay exercise.

The Recall

Start with your dog in the Sit-Stay, with the twenty-five-foot lead attached to her collar. Bring the lead out to her right or left side a few inches before stretching it out away from her. This is important to remember, so that your dog won't step on the lead when you call her to you. If your dog steps on the lead as she starts to come to you, she will feel the tug of it and stop, because she will think you are correcting her. If the lead is properly positioned, once your dog goes into motion the lead will trail behind her as she comes toward you. If she does happen to step on it, the tug won't be as noticeable to her as it would be if the lead were directly in front of her when she stepped forward.

Give the command "Come." As your dog responds, be sure she doesn't come in on an angle. If she begins to head toward either side, don't try to reel in the long lead. Command "No," go to your dog and make the correction by putting on the six-foot lead and repeating the command "Come." With the short lead you can correct the angle of your dog's approach and then go back to working with the long lead.

When your dog comes to you and sits directly in front of you, you can bring her to the Heel position in one of two ways:

1. Take up some of the slack of the long lead by picking up the lead in your left hand, then give the command to heel.

2. Unsnap the long lead and snap on the grab lead. Command your dog to heel and hold the grab lead only if you need to make a correction.

Once you and your dog are comfortable working with the intermediate lead, look for some distractions. Take her to an area where she might see another animal or other distraction while she is doing the Recall. Find out whether you can control her when you are farther away from her. Let her out the full length of the lead, put her in a Sit-Stay and then call her to you. If she's preoccupied and doesn't come back to you, all you have to do is move your hands toward the dog to get some slack in the long lead, step back and give the lead a good yank to make it tighten up on the dog's collar as you correct her by saying "No!" sharply. Release your grip on the lead immediately, just as if you were snapping and releasing a standard lead. Do this until you feel you have complete control over your dog, regardless of what the distraction may be.

18

The Crepe Paper Test

THE FINAL PREPARATION for working off lead is the Crepe Paper Test. It is the most foolproof way I know to evaluate accomplishments and pinpoint weak spots. If your dog makes a mistake and you have to correct him, the paper will break. There are no possible excuses.

Your dog will notice the difference immediately because the weight of the crepe paper will be lighter. But he will realize that you can still control him. You, however, will feel at a disadvantage, because you know the paper won't hold him if he decides to break your command. You will have to rely on your past training. If you worked on the mechanics properly, you will be able to pass the Crepe Paper Test. If you didn't demand enough of yourself and your dog, you will fail.

The Mechanics

Use the kind of crepe paper that comes on a roll. Cut off a strip as long as your lead, plus a few more inches so you can tie one end onto your dog's collar and hold the other end in your hand.

With the paper tied to your dog's collar, go through all the basic exercises just as if you were using the leather lead. By this time, you should be making your corrections automatically, without even thinking about them. For instance, when you are doing the About-Turn and you see that your dog isn't keeping up with you as you make the turn, you will snap the paper—and it will break. Cut a new strip of paper and begin again.

This test will show you how stable your dog is under command. If you can spend an hour going through the exercise without breaking the paper, then you are ready to begin doing the exercises off lead. If the paper breaks, you will see exactly where you need to do more work.

By the time you take this test, your dog should be able to perform all the exercises, without any corrections, even when there are distractions. It is okay for you to begin using crepe paper in a quiet area, but you should then go on to busy areas such as playgrounds and shopping centers.

If the dog breaks the crepe paper, don't be discouraged. Ask yourself *why* the dog broke the paper. Go back to your six-foot lead and find out what you are doing wrong. If you didn't spend enough time repeating the exercise when you first began to do it, if your dog's response didn't become automatic, this is when it will show up.

19

Totally Off Lead

TAKING THE GRAB LEAD OFF

Although taking the grab lead off your dog may seem like a minor step, it can be very stressful for you. At this point your dog will probably be relaxed and ready to obey your commands, but all of a sudden you realize that if he breaks, you have no way to control him.

This is the time to pay close attention to your voice, as you should have been doing from the beginning. This, along with all the training you have done, constitutes your authority. Give your commands confidently and your dog will respond in the same way. It is just as if your manner were traveling down the lead to your dog. If you can't keep your anxiety out of your voice, go back to the grab lead—or even the six-foot lead.

Working without any lead is a very dramatic step for you to take. When you were working with the lead over your shoulder or around your waist, or with the grab lead or the strip of crepe paper, your dog was not mechanically connected to you. But now he is not connected to you psychologically either. He has no physical reminder of your control over him. And you have nothing to grab except the dog himself, should anything happen—and he can move faster than you can.

Working off lead, gradually build up distance between you and your dog

When you get to this phase, proceed as you did with the lead over your shoulder and with the grab lead. Go through all the basic exercises. Work quietly at first. Then build in some distractions. When you and your dog can work confidently in the face of any and all distractions, when you know that your dog will respond to each and every command that you give him, you are ready for a very special test of your authority.

TAKING THE COLLAR OFF

Taking the collar off is a special test of your abilities. Actually, it's another proof of your accomplishments. At this point in my classes I tell my students to take the collars off their dogs. Usually I am greeted with gasps of disbelief. "No," I always say, "I'm serious. Now you have nothing to depend on but yourself."

If you think this is an impossible goal for you to achieve, imagine how you would feel in a class of twenty other people and dogs, all of them going through the exercises without even collars on the dogs. Yet I've never been disappointed in the results.

When you have no physical control over your dog, and no way to hold onto him if he breaks, you have to give your commands with authority. You have to pay attention to your voice. If you are uncertain, don't let it show. Don't say to yourself, "I don't have the lead, I don't even have the collar—I can't control this dog!" Instead, let your authority tell your dog, "If you are going to break, I am still going to correct you." Command the dog to heel as if you know very well he will obey—and he will. Let your voice communicate your confidence to your dog in the same way the lead once did.

After you discover that your dog will obey even though he isn't wearing a collar, you will have to put it back on to comply with most leash laws. But, if you choose, you can leave the collar off when your dog is in your home.

20

Raising Your Level of Training

BY NOW you should know how your dog ought to perform when you give him a command. When he doesn't perform well, set aside some time to work on the problem. If everything is going well, review all the basic exercises—on lead, with the crepe paper and off lead—about once a month. This will vary with the dog. Sometimes once a week will be better.

Training doesn't end. You and your dog have gone through the formal exercises, but now it is time to put your formal training to practical use. You can have fun doing it, too.

When you are taking a walk with your dog and letting him exercise his curiosity, occasionally command him to heel. If you are in a wooded area, weave him around a few trees. If you are in a crowded business area, weave around people. Put your dog in a Sit-Stay while you throw a ball and then let him fetch it. While you are having a good time you can also check up on your dog's performance. When you have him on a Heel command, walk straight toward a wall and suddenly do an About-Turn. Does your dog stop and pull back from the wall, or does he go with you? Does he stay in line with your left leg when you turn? Put your training into your ordinary, everyday life.

THE SOCIABLE DOG

A sociable dog is nothing more than a well-trained dog that is exposed to people and other animals. Don't put your dog away when you have guests. Let him join the party.

The exposure should begin when the dog is a puppy. Put him on a lead for a while when visitors come to your house. You can still talk to your guests while you are holding the lead. If your puppy is shy, you can use a baby gate to close off part of a room so that your dog can be with you and at the same time out of the way. Let him see what is going on and encourage your guests to go over and talk to him. When he feels more comfortable, you can bring him in closer on a lead.

If your dog is *very* shy, don't put him in another part of the room behind a gate because the gate will only reinforce his tendency to withdraw from people. In such a case, it's better to keep your dog with you, in close contact with your guests.

When people arrive, you dog will probably get excited. This is perfectly normal. Allow him some time to become familiar with your guests and he will soon calm down. Make your corrections if he does something wrong or makes a pest of himself. This is how he learns how to behave with other people.

By now your dog knows what he can and cannot do among family members. Be sure he follows the same rules with guests. But here you may have to correct the guests instead of the dog. For example, suppose you are in the habit of watching television at night while you enjoy a snack. Your dog may be sitting close by, but he won't touch your food because you have corrected him when he tried that, and you have reinforced that rule many times. But now your best friend is visiting you and trying to slip your dog a piece of cheese when you are not looking. If that happens, don't correct your dog. If someone offers him something good to eat, he is going to take it. But that is the end of your rules. Correct your friend. Explain that you don't want your dog to get in the habit of stealing food—and that is what will happen if you don't reinstate the rules.

When you go to visit friends, take your dog with you as often as you can. But always ask your friends if it is all right for you to bring him. If your friends are willing to help you expose your dog to new environments, be considerate of them. Keep your dog on a lead, especially if he is a puppy, until he settles down. If your friends do not want him exploring their home, keep him close to you. If he knows the Sit-Stay or the Down-Stay command, use it. Don't take your puppy visiting unless he is housebroken. If your dog gets up on a chair, ask your friends if they object. If they say yes, don't be offended. Tell your dog to get off the chair. It is your friends' house, and their rules.

21

Keeping Your Dog Fit

FITNESS IS AS IMPORTANT to your dog as it is to you. If your dog is trained, it is easier for you to keep him in good shape, because you can use your commands to exercise him. You don't need a lot of space or fancy equipment. All you need is a little ingenuity in making use of your environment.

Exercise, to be effective, should be done routinely, a certain number of times a week, for specific lengths of time. But that doesn't mean you can't have fun while you are doing it. Look around and see what you can do with some ordinary objects.

JUMPING

Most dogs love to jump, and it is very easy to train them. You don't need regulation hurdles, either. Set a picnic table or a bench on its side. If you live in the city and don't have much recreational space, take a few cardboard boxes to the park or a courtyard and use them as a broad jump.

Use your basic training to teach your dog how to go over a hurdle. Start with the lead and work your way up to off lead. Begin with him at your side in a Sit, facing the hurdle. Give the command to heel and begin running toward the hurdle. As you approach it, give the command "Over" or "Jump," hold the lead up so it won't get in your dog's way and, at the very last moment, pass the hurdle on the right side while your dog jumps over the middle. When your dog comes down on the other side, go back into a Heel, then an About-Turn and end in a Heel position facing the hurdle. Remember to praise your dog.

Another way to do it is to put your dog in a Sit-Stay on one side of the hurdle while you stand facing him on the other. The lead should be over the top of the hurdle. Go back to your Recall exercise for this: Call your dog's name, hesitate and give the command to come. Snap the lead upward as you give the command and begin to go backward.

When your dog jumps the hurdle, keep running backward for a short distance and then stop. Your dog should stop in a Sit directly in front of you. Command her to heel beside you, take a step forward and complete the exercise. Your dog won't even know she is being trained. She will just be having fun. But don't skip the praise.

The broad jump is similar, except that you will be concentrating on the width of the jump rather than the height. Set up two small, low cardboard boxes a few inches apart. Gradually move them farther apart to widen the jump. The width will depend upon the size and breed of your dog.

Begin in the same way, with your dog beside you in a Sit and the lead in your right hand. Give the Heel command and run toward the boxes. As you approach them, give the command "Over" or "Jump," lift the lead slightly to get it out of your dog's way when she jumps and pass the boxes on the right side while your dog jumps across the middle.

A few words of advice about jumping. Remember, this is exercise, not competition. It doesn't matter how high your dog jumps or how far. What matters is the conditioning of his body. If he has to strain to clear a hurdle or span an obstacle, he may hurt himself. If he falls down, he may be injured. Urge him to exercise, but don't push him too far. Your goal is to condition your dog, not set records.

Formal hurdles . . .

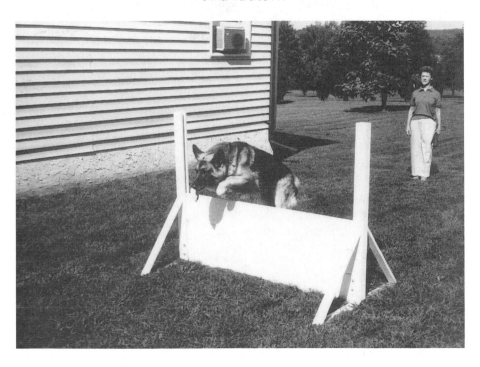

PLAYING BALL

Most dogs love to run after a ball. Not all dogs will bring it back. Most of them have to be taught, and that is part of retrieving, which is a book in itself.

If your dog likes to play ball and brings it back to you, work some of your commands into the game. Tell him to sit and then stay while you throw the ball. Wait a few seconds before you send him after it, allowing his excitement to build up. When he runs after it and picks it up, command him to come.

Look for other objects to throw—sticks or some of his toys— and let him bring them back.

CITY DOGS

Dogs that live in the city have to exercise in small spaces and sometimes indoors. If you have a small dog, you can exercise him in your apartment.

It isn't a good idea to have your dog jump over obstacles on hard surfaces, such as concrete or even a wooden floor. Your dog needs something to absorb the shock of jumping and coming down on a hard surface. One of the best shock absorbers is a runner—a long, narrow piece of carpet with a thick underpad glued to the bottom of it.

Put the runner down in the middle of a room, away from furniture that might be knocked over. Or, if you have a long hallway, put it down there. Place small boxes on top of the runner as a broad jump or use them separately as hurdles.

If there is nothing but concrete outdoors, take the runner out with you. It may be rather bulky for one person to carry, but perhaps you can team up with a neighbor who wants to exercise his dog and will help you carry the equipment.

SWIMMING

If you know of a place where your dog can swim, by all means take him there. Swimming is a wonderful exercise for dogs as well as people, and most dogs love it.

. . . or picnic tables and benches

Introduce your dog to the water gradually. Don't throw him in a lake and expect him to be happy about it. Let him approach the water at his own pace. Go along with him. Once he enjoys the cooling effects, he will know what to do.

A FEW CAVEATS

About Frisbees. I realize how appealing a Frisbee game looks on all those television commercials showing dogs jumping high up into the air to retrieve them. But consider the dog. When a dog hurls his body up into the air, his body twists and turns. He may catch the Frisbee, but he also stands a good chance of twisting his stomach and his intestines. This can cause serious injuries. He may also suffer injuries to his back.

Another point to consider is that when your dog jumps for a Frisbee, he will come down hard on his hind legs. In fact, all his weight may come down on them, and he may injure his hips. If he comes down on his front legs, he may injure his shoulders. These are some of the reasons I don't play Frisbee with my dogs.

About running. If you are a runner, consider leaving your dog at home when you exercise. When you run, you wear special shoes to absorb the shock of your foot coming down on a hard surface continually over a long period of time. You can stop and get a drink, and when you come home you can jump in the shower to cool off.

Your dog can't do any of these things. He doesn't have sneakers or running shoes. He can't get a drink as easily as you can. He probably can't cool off in the shower. And it is harder for his body to cool down to a normal temperature. If you would like to slow down to a walk, then take your dog along.

There may be some exceptions: if the climate is agreeable; if the surface is soft, such as grass; and if the dog is in condition, having run with you over a period of time and he has gradually built up his endurance; the exercise should not hurt him.

Afterword

CONGRATULATIONS! You now have a trained dog, and I'm sure you're beginning to realize what the advantages are. If not, just compare what your dog can do now with what he couldn't do when you got him, and you'll see how much the two of you have accomplished together: You're both working off lead in all kinds of circumstances, and you're comfortable doing it.

Looking to the future, you may choose to go on to higher degrees of accomplishment. Whether you do or don't, however, there are two important rules for you to remember: *Don't get lazy* and *don't get stagnant*. If you want to make the most out of your training, follow these guidelines:

Don't keep repeating only the exercises you have already learned—try some variations.

Don't go through the exercises mechanically—do them enthusiastically.

Don't take your dog to the same places all the time—look for new environments.

Whenever practical, take your dog with you wherever you go. New challenges come up all the time; they're good for you and good for your dog.

Bibliography

For information on breed characteristics, the following publications are recommended:
The Complete Dog Book (The Official Publication of the American Kennel Club), latest edition, Howell Book House

Periodicals:
Dog World (Annual Edition), Maclean Hunter Publishing Corp., 29 N. Wacker Drive, Chicago, IL 60606-3298
Dogs USA, Fancy Publications, Inc., 3 Burroughs, Irvine, CA 92718